Raised
QUILT AND STITCH

Dedication

I dedicate this book to my long-suffering husband Ron, who has endured everything that my life as a designer and teacher has thrown at him for over forty years now.

To my lovely daughters Sharon and Lisa, I would like to express my thanks for your continued encouragement, patience and love throughout the process of creating this book. Also to my lovely grandsons Luke and Jack, and my granddaughter Isis, who have recently extended our family and have brought so much joy and fun into our lives. To my sons-in-law Antony and Simon who have unwittingly become part of their 'odd' mother-in-law's life! Thanks for all that you do. I love you all.

There are so many others who have helped and supported me along the way throughout my life – past and present.
This is for you.

Foreword

I first met Sylvia as her tutor in the early years of the City & Guilds Patchwork and Quilting courses at Bromley Adult Education Centre. She brought to the classes a wide range of competencies and artistic skills along with her enthusiasm for learning, and was always among the most innovative with her ideas and design work. From her many accomplishments she has built an expertise across the quilting world, and is particularly known for her corded and stuffed work. I have seen her at many quilt exhibitions and events demonstrating her unique method of quilting. Through teaching, talks and workshops countrywide she is encouraging others to enjoy quilting. She works as a judge co-ordinator at national shows and has published a number of magazine articles. All these talents and abilities are brought into the content of this book, which illustrates the fun of quiltmaking.

Pat Salt

Pat Salt is best known for her contribution to bringing quiltmaking to education by the development of the pilot courses for both parts of the City & Guilds Patchwork and Quilting qualification, and in designing the first distance learning programme for the courses. She is a practising quiltmaker, show judge and lecturer with particular interest in experimental techniques and the wider advancement of the craft.

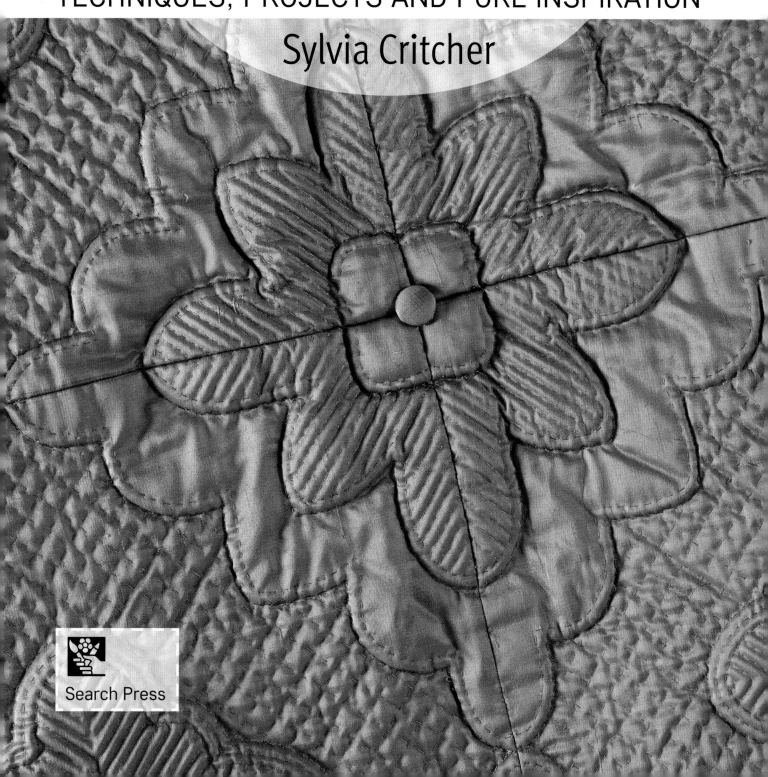

Raised
QUILT AND STITCH

TECHNIQUES, PROJECTS AND PURE INSPIRATION

Sylvia Critcher

Search Press

First published in 2016

Search Press Limited
Wellwood, North Farm Road,
Tunbridge Wells, Kent TN2 3DR

Text and templates copyright © Sylvia Critcher 2016

Photographs by Roddy Paine Photographic Studio

Photographs and design copyright © Search Press Ltd.
2016

Illustrations by Michael Yeowell at Blue Rabbit

ISBN: 978-1-78221-014-6

The Publishers and author can accept no responsibility for
any consequences arising from the information, advice or
instructions given in this publication.

Suppliers
If you have difficulty in obtaining any of the materials and
equipment mentioned in this book, then please visit the
Search Press website for details of suppliers:
www.searchpress.com

You are invited to visit the author's website to view
further work, patterns and templates, and links to suitable
suppliers of materials and equipment specific
to this book: www.sylviacritcher.co.uk

Printed in China

*Detail from a 1920s housecoat in peach crêpe de
Chine. It was given to the author by Maria-
Luisa Boldori, from Italy. The piece features
Italian quilting and was designed and made by
Maria-Luisa's mother for her own trousseau.*

Acknowledgements

Very special thanks to Gill Rathbone for her
generosity of time for testing out so many of my
patterns to the detriment of completing her own
quilt this year! Also to Sue Irwin, Anita Gallo and
Val Crooks, without whose help with some of the
stitching I could not have completed some of the
projects on time. Thanks to my quilt group,
Hope Quilters, who have cheered me on during the
writing of this book or have 'done a bit of stitching'
for me on the inspirational section.

Sincere thanks to my quilters who kindly loaned their
quilts to be photographed: Sue Irwin, Chris Parker,
Anita Gallo, Jean Witherick, Sen Arpino and
Barbara Cox, and to my friend Annie Summerhayes
who is always there for me and willing to try out
some of my wackier quilting ideas.

To Pat Salt and Dinah Travis who first introduced
le boutis technique to me.

My gratitude goes to Maria-Luisa Boldori for her gift
of her mother's Italian quilted housecoat, which I will
treasure, and to Jane from Lincolnshire who gave me
her mother's Italian quilting cushion kit.

Very special thanks to Kim Shaw for the loan of her
exquisite piece of original *le boutis* work.

To Roddy Paine for all his patience and commitment
during the photoshoot as well as for his stunning
photography. Thanks also go to little Ozzy for
assisting in the process!

My appreciation to Roger Cooling at
Grosvenor Shows Ltd, for his continued support
over the years, and for allowing me to showcase my
techniques all around the UK. Also to
Emma Cooling (former editor of *Fabrications*
magazine) for all her encouragement and belief in me
for the years we worked together. To Val Nesbitt and
her team at Justhands-on.tv who also encourage and
promote all that I do worldwide.

Finally, I would like to thank Katie French and
Becky Shackleton together with the team at
Search Press for their belief in me and making my
ideas become reality – I am forever in your debt.

Contents

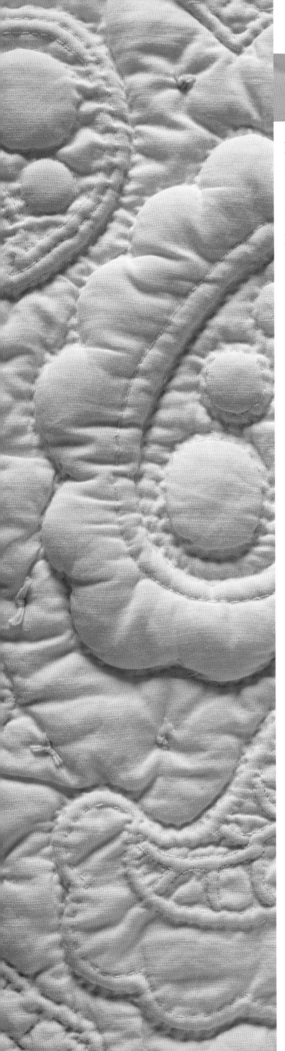

Introduction

I have lost count of the number of times I have been asked if there is a book on the technique that has become my signature style. Or of the number of people who have asked me, 'is it trapunto?' or tell me, 'it looks so complicated, I could never master it!' I hope this book answers your questions and encourages you on your way to creativity.

Little did I know that making a 21 x 30cm (8^1/$_3$ x 11^2/$_3$in) teaching sample to illustrate the possibility of combining Italian quilting, trapunto and French *boutis* would become such an important milestone in my career (see images left and right, and in full on page 124). When it was initially completed, I looked at it and saw the potential for a pillow pattern – my plan was to mirror image the initial design, rotate it and look at the result – words that I often use in class to encourage students to explore their own ideas. But the pillow was never made. Curiosity in these newly combined techniques had got the better of me, and instead the quilt 'Symphony 2000' – a double bed-sized quilt – evolved from the sample (see pages 124–125).

I had been invited to demonstrate at the Grosvenor national quilt shows in 1997, following the success of 'Thank You Charlie', a quilt that I had made and exhibited in 1996. I needed something to work on at the shows, so what better than the new quilt? It would be very different in technique but it would all be hand-stitched and ideal to take with me. I had decided to make it using the 'quilt-as-you-go' method. The centre panel would be made first, then the borders added – at that time a new departure from the familiar quilt-as-you-go blocks.

At one show, early in 1998, whilst working on the centre panel, I was asked how long it would take to complete and so foolishly I said, 'this will be my Millennium quilt!' Given that I was teaching full time – plus evenings and some weekends – it was a bit stupid to make such a rash statement and the weeks flew by faster than I would have liked. By the time the 1999 deadline arrived I had the centre panel and the first borders completed and I was still working on the final borders – there was no way it was going to be ready in time, so I opted for completing the quilt at this stage and planned to add the borders later. Needless to say the borders are still waiting to be added to the quilt and the saying 'never put off till tomorrow what you should do today' haunts me on a regular basis. I am still determined, though, that the final borders will be added in the near future!

Several of the students I was teaching at that time wanted to know if they could try out the technique I had used, and with my guidance, they set about making small quilts of their own. These subsequently were invited to be shown together with my quilt at the spring quilt fairs in 2000. I was on hand to explain about the techniques I had used and had a small demonstration piece to work on – a corner design taken from my quilt. It's strange how fate takes a hand, as this became the pillow 'Ivory Inspiration', which was made at very short notice for the *Crafts Beautiful* magazine spring supplement. '"Ivory Inspiration": cording and stuffing – with a difference' had arrived and was a great success.

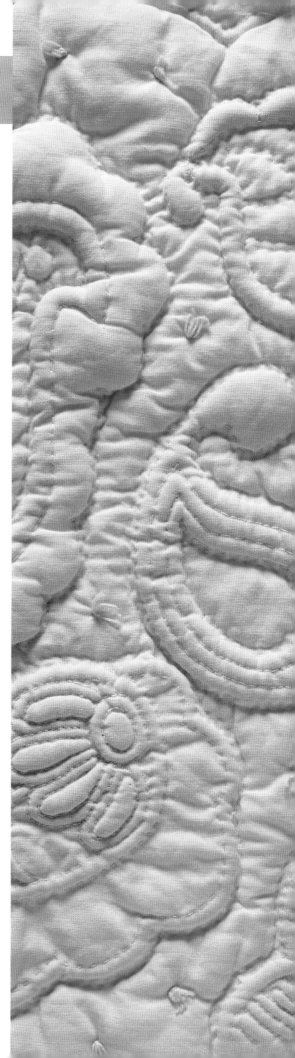

With the positive feedback from the general public and, by request, the other patterns and workshops have evolved taking me all over the UK and to both the USA and Spain. At the time, I had no idea how this would develop or that over ten years later it would still be as popular as ever. I think too that I came to the quilt shows with a different hand-stitching technique at just the right time. During the late 1990s, machine quilting had become the latest technique within the patchwork and quilting world and had really taken off in a big way – long gone were the days when 'machine quilting' was unacceptable – how fashions change and contradict! Most quilts were being machined to excess and traditional hand-stitching started to take a back seat. As I travelled around the UK, many people would tell me that there was nothing new for hand quilters, and that they felt neglected in the current machine-orientated climate, and in part this was true. My solution was just a case of looking at what had gone before, re-visiting it and giving it a bit of a makeover... then being brave enough to have a go.

The techniques that I have revived had almost disappeared. Their prior popularity had lasted until the late 1950s and mid-1960s, when Italian quilting was in vogue. It was usually stitched on brightly coloured satins and made into handkerchief and nightdress cases, pillows and decorative bed jackets. With the introduction of central heating, the rise in popularity of tissues over handkerchiefs, and the fact that many women started to return to full-time work after having children, the need for such items disappeared and the time-consuming hand-stitched techniques fell out of favour. When polyester wadding (batting) arrived from the USA it changed traditional quilting and gave quilt-making a much needed boost.

So what makes my work so different? The techniques are all traditional, but I have given them a new slant – re-vamped the tradition and simplified part of the process. I have combined them together and added traditional English quilting and knotting to the mix, plus some additional forms of embellishment. This gives the work a very three-dimensional, textured outcome that appears to be ultra-complicated, but it is in fact very easy to do – in part this is an optical illusion through stitch! I have been demonstrating my three-dimensional quilting all over the UK, Europe and the USA for many years now. Although I teach and enjoy all aspects of patchwork and quilting, my love for this technique has never left me and I continue to create new designs and patterns and explore variations using the technique. Further ideas are springing to mind; development and experimentation are looming on the horizon... keeping this technique alive is high on my agenda.

I have just one final thing to add: beware – this work can become totally addictive. So do not blame me when the potatoes are well and truly welded to the bottom of the saucepan, and the carrots carry that strange brown tinge and acquire a rather odd taste. Trust me, the family will get used to it!

Sylvia

The images left and right show my paisley design, which inspired my development of the raised quilting and stitching techniques. See also page 124.

Basic techniques

All the quilting techniques I use can be traced back to the Middle Ages. Many historical quilted items have been found from all around the world – some of these pieces can be found in museums and are in excellent condition having been valued as heirlooms or owned by the aristocracy. I have combined several key traditional techniques in my raised quilting designs – I use trapunto stuffed work, Italian corded work, French-style cording (my adaptation of *le boutis*) and English quilting. All other additional techniques will be explained where necessary when linked to the projects. In order to understand the work, it is a good idea to familiarise yourself with each technique in its traditional form – I have illustrated this with one design that shows each outcome. Although it sounds complicated, it is very easy to do. If you can sew a running stitch, you will be able to do this work. Each technique can be used in its own right or combined with others. I am using my 'Solo' pincushion design to illustrate all except the *le boutis* technique.

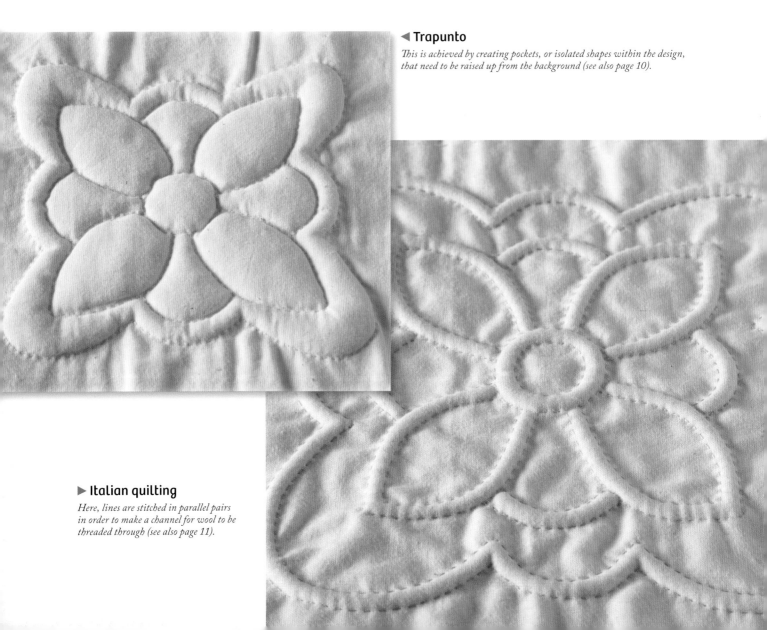

◀ **Trapunto**
This is achieved by creating pockets, or isolated shapes within the design, that need to be raised up from the background (see also page 10).

▶ **Italian quilting**
Here, lines are stitched in parallel pairs in order to make a channel for wool to be threaded through (see also page 11).

▲ Le boutis

Shown above is the centre detail of a typical French motif. Every area of the design is corded and stuffed with cotton thread and fibres. The design is completely reversible (see also pages 12–13).

▲ French-style cording

This is my version of le boutis, it appears to be the same from the front but it does not need to be reversible (see also page 14).

▲ English quilting

A layer of wadding (batting) is sandwiched between two layers of fabric, held together with lines of stitching (see also page 15).

▶ Combining techniques

Here is my 'Solo' design, which is made up of the four techniques (trapunto, Italian quilting, French-style cording and English quilting), giving a highly three-dimensional, textured outcome to the final piece. The left side of the piece shows the final quilting in place – the right side is ready for the final quilting.

Trapunto

This is sometimes referred to as stuffed work. It is used to add another dimension to a quilted fabric – it is a puffy, decorative feature that gives a unique, embossed texture. This high-relief technique is worked through at least two layers of cloth; you will outline the design in running stitch before padding it from the underside with man-made or natural fibres.

To work trapunto: draw the design onto the right side of the fabric. Place the open-weave material to the back of the work. Tack (baste) the two fabrics together. Sew all along the drawn lines with small running stitch through both layers of fabric. The stitched areas are creating pockets. Turn the work to the wrong side in order to work the next stage. Remove the tacking (basting) stitches from the stitched areas. Make a small hole into the centre of each pocket shape, through the open-weave fabric only, and part the fibres. Be very careful not to cut through to the front of the work. Tease out the toy filler into small wispy amounts and carefully fill the shape using the stuffing stick or tweezers to help. Do not over-stuff the shape or it will pucker and distort the surrounding fabric. If necessary, sew up the hole with ladder stitch or herringbone stitch, to prevent the filling working its way out. Do not pull the threads too tightly together or this will also distort the finish. The design will appear slightly raised on the right side of the work and create a shadow. Fill any remaining pockets in the same way. Use for obscure or isolated shapes when it is not suitable to include double lines within a design.

Materials required

- Plain cotton fabric for the front (right side) of the work
- English butter muslin (cheesecloth) or fine open-weave fabric for the backing fabric
- Polyester toy filler (or shredded-up polyester wadding/batting), for raising the design
- Sewing thread
- Tweezers, or stuffing stick
- Small scissors

DICTIONARY DEFINITION

Italian, from *trapungere:* to embroider.
Latin, from *pungere:* to prick with a needle.

The embossed effect created on the right side of the work. The shadows created by the raised shapes are clearly visible.

The back of the work – some of the holes have been stitched up with herringbone stitch.

Italian quilting

This technique is also known as corded work. It was especially popular in Italian clothing between 1920 and 1925.

The completed right side of the work.

Materials required

- Plain cotton fabric for the front (right side) of the work
- English butter muslin (cheesecloth) or fine open-weave fabric for the backing fabric
- Quilting wool, or other suitable knitting wool, for threading and lifting the design
- Sewing thread
- A large-eyed, round-ended needle for threading the wool

DICTIONARY DEFINITION

Parallel lines of stitching about 3–5mm (⅛–¼in) apart, worked on two layers of fabric in running stitch or backstitch. Threaded with yarn from the wrong side of the work.

To work Italian quilting: draw the design with double lines onto the right side of the fabric. Add the open-weave material to the back of the work. Tack (baste) together. Sew all along the drawn lines with small running stitches. This will create channels. Remove the tacking (basting) stitches within the stitched areas. Turn the work over to the back. Thread a large-eyed blunt-ended needle with a 50cm (20in) length of the quilting wool. Proceed to part the loose fibres of the muslin (cheesecloth) fabric and make a hole with the needle large enough to thread the wool through one of the channels. Approximately every 5cm (2in) remove the needle from the channel, pull the wool gently through, then return the needle back into the *same* hole and thread the wool back into the channel. Leave a small loop at each exit point. Follow around the channel to complete the shape. At the beginning and end of each channel leave a short tail, about 5mm (¼in) projecting from the work and then cut off. This will allow for any shrinkage of the wool during laundering. Continue in this way until all the channels are filled.

Using pre-shrunk wool showing small loops and tails left on the wrong side.

GENERAL ADVICE FOR LEAVING TAILS AND LOOPS

Tails: leave these projecting by approximately 5mm (¼in) at the beginning and end of each channel – or when joining new wool to the channel.

Loops: these should be worked on small curved shapes. Remove the wool from the channel and then thread it back into the same hole leaving about a 5mm (¼in) loop remaining on the surface of the butter muslin (cheesecloth). Also leave loops at corners and points in a design – this will make a good sharp effect from the right side and will prevent the design having 'empty' corners. Loops should be left every 12cm (5in) on long continuous designs, unless you are using a pre-shrunk wool – then you need only leave the loops at corners, or at points within a design: 'top of hills or bottom of valleys' is a guide for remembering where these should be.

This unfinished 1950s Italian quilted pillow kit is a great example of this technique. The iron-on transfer on the coarse, open-weave backing fabric is visible. You can see the numerous shrinkage loops of the wool on the back of the work.

11

Le boutis

Also known as French cording, Marseilles quilting or Broderie de Marseille, *le boutis* originated in the Provence region of France during the 1400s. This high-class silk needlework was exported to England and the rest of Europe, to royalty and the aristocracy. By the 17th and 18th centuries the region's main exports were the sumptuous, intricately designed whitework bed covers, quilts and *petassouns*. Many of the fine white cotton fabrics used – mousseline or cambresine – were imported in huge quantities from India and around five thousand women were employed in the factories in France. The traditional French sample shown here was made in about 1890, and was purchased at a market in Nîmes, north of Marseilles.

To work *le boutis*: tack (baste) both fabrics together. Draw your design onto one side of the work, but create parallel channels of design that are approximately 3mm (¹/₈in) apart; these may be straight or curved lines. Usually the entire background is covered with lines too. Stitch along each line with matching sewing thread and very small stitches to create channels. Ensure that the stitches are identical on both sides of the work as the back is as important as the front. Work from the back. Thread the needle with the yarn and carefully part the fibres of the channels. Proceed to thread every channel with the cotton yarn. At the end of each channel, cut the yarn off as close to the channel as possible and tease the fabric fibres back together. You do not need to leave loops or tails, as the cotton yarn will not need the shrinkage allowance. Stuff areas of the design with small chopped-up pieces of the cotton thread – or a cotton filling. Again, part the fibres to stuff and invisibly close the hole as before. This work needs to be totally reversible. Thread every row with the cotton yarn to give a surface of multiple raised channels across the entire piece. The very beautiful intricate designs are usually finished with scalloped edges or handmade gathered Broderie Anglaise.

Materials required

- Two white cotton fabrics of the same size and type
- *Le boutis* cotton yarn for threading
- Sewing thread
- A large-eyed, round-ended needle

DICTIONARY DEFINITION

Boutis is the Provençal word both for high-relief corded and quilted petticoats and bed covers, and also for the round-ended needle used to thread the cording through the channels.

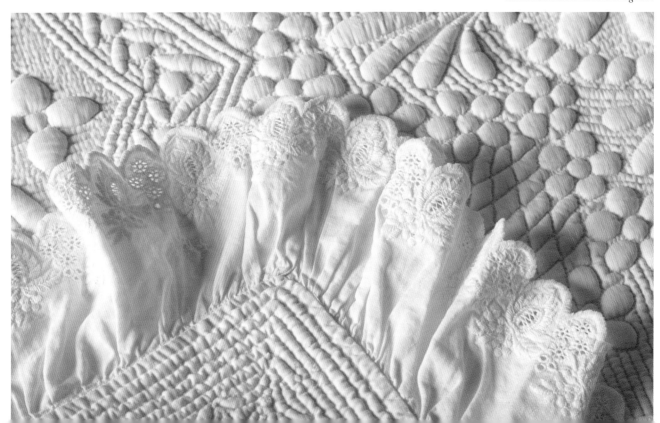

The gathered edge finish features this incredibly delicate handmade Broderie Anglaise.

Here you can see the entire piece. This le boutis *item is probably a* petassoun *– a small lap quilt made to protect clothing from baby dribble and other spills when holding an infant. It was kindly loaned to me by Kim Shaw.*

In this detail you can see the wrong side of the work in the foreground, with the right side above and towards the top right.

13

French-style cording

This is my version of *le boutis*. Once I discovered *le boutis* quilting, it did not take long to realise that, although very attractive, it was very time-consuming to carry out, and I could not contemplate using it over large areas. For this reason I have the utmost respect for the French quilts made in this style as they are very labour-intensive. Looking at my options for re-creating this style visually, and with the knowledge that I would be covering the back of my work, I decided that I would treat it in the same way as Italian quilting but just add far more lines to completely cover the area of the design. I adopted the name 'French-style quilting' as it was not true *le boutis*, but visually simulated the style from the right side of the work.

To work French-style cording: draw the design on the right side of the fabric but add additional lines to form extra channels that will cover the background material – I like to use strips of masking tape to ensure evenly spaced lines. Place the open-weave material to the back of the work. Tack (baste) the two fabrics together. Sew along the drawn lines with a small running stitch, ensuring that every line is stitched so there are no spaces between the channels. Remove the tacking (basting) stitches and working from the back, thread the wool into every channel until the whole design is complete (see Italian quilting on page 11). Leave loops and tails as for Italian quilting.

Materials required

- Plain cotton fabric for the front (right side) of the work
- English butter muslin (cheesecloth) or fine open-weave fabric for the backing fabric
- Quilting wool, or other suitable knitting wool, for threading and lifting the design
- Sewing thread
- A large-eyed, round-ended needle for threading the wool

The right side of the completed work with every channel threaded.

The back of the work. I used pre-shrunk wool, which requires fewer loops and tails.

English quilting

Most of you will be familiar with this technique, but I have included it just in case there are novice quilters wanting to make some of the projects. Modern quilting uses a variety of fibres for the wadding (batting) depending on the use.

To work English quilting: draw your design onto the front of one of the fabrics. Place this on top of the wadding (batting) and use the second fabric as the backing. This is a 'quilt sandwich'. Tack (baste) the three layers together and stitch through all layers with a running stitch, or backstitch to hold the fabrics together. The knot at the beginning and end of the stitching should be hidden between the layers of fabric and not be visible from either side of the work. Both sides should appear the same. This gives the 'quilted' effect. It is also possible to transfer your design onto the quilt sandwich once the three layers are together.

Materials required

- Two white cotton fabrics of the same size and type
- Wadding (batting) cut slightly larger all round than the fabrics
- Sewing or quilting thread

DICTIONARY DEFINITION

A coverlet or blanket made of two layers of fabric with a layer of cotton, wool, feathers or down in between. All stitched firmly together, usually with a criss-cross design. Latin, from *culcita*: meaning bolster or pillow. Middle English, from *quilte*: meaning a sack filled with feathers.

The 'Solo' design, worked using English quilting.

Getting started

If you are already familiar with sewing, you will no doubt have your own range of equipment. You do not need to purchase lots of expensive tools in order to create the three-dimensional raised stitching. I have listed the necessities, which will also provide a guide for those who are just beginning to embark on quilting.

Equipment

CUTTING MAT, ROTARY CUTTER AND RULER

These items have changed the way that fabric is cut – making it fast and easy. If you are a novice, it may be worthwhile having some professional instruction in using them.

Cutting mat: there are a number of brands of self-healing cutting mats – buy a good quality one. A3 (29.7 x 42cm / 11¾ x 16½in) is the best starting size, with both metric and imperial measurements. Later you might like to add an A2 (42 x 59.4cm / 16½ x 23½in) mat to your set.

Rulers: these are non-slip, transparent and available in a variety of widths and with metric and/or imperial measurements. Purchase the ruler that matches the size of the mat – select one that is longer rather than shorter.

Rotary cutter: there are many different styles and sizes available, so if you can, try before you buy. Beware, as this is a very sharp tool – think of it as a circular razor blade. Always cut away from you and remember to replace the blade guard after each use. Keep well away from children. Replacement blades are available; discard old blades sensibly.

MARKING TOOLS

Pencil: I use a basic, sharpened HB pencil for marking out my designs on paper and for transferring them onto fabric; a propelling (automatic) HB pencil can also be used.

Dressmakers' chalk: (in pencil form if possible) is useful for marking darker fabrics – in white, yellow, pink or blue.

Eraser: some are produced for fabric but do not always work. This is trial and error – if you have transferred your design onto fabric with a pencil, providing you have not made them too dark, the marks will disappear as you stitch. I find that a Magic Eraser block can be useful used dry, and pencil erasers from high street stores work equally well. There are other marking tools available, but I do not favour them as the long-term chemical damage to fabric is unknown.

MASKING TAPE

This is one item that you cannot do without. I use it as a guide to mark out additional lines of stitching (see page 35). It comes in a variety of widths and grades of stickiness referred to as 'tack'. You will need the 'low-tack' variety in both 5mm (¼in) and 1cm (½in) widths. Low-tack tape will have enough adhesive to stick to your fabric but will not leave a residue of glue on your work. Each piece of tape can be re-used at least three times. Some stores sell it as 'zebra' tape – this is striped and used to help with stitch length. You can also buy curved tape, but it isn't essential.

SCISSORS

Purchase good-quality scissors and treat them with respect – if you look after your scissors they will last for years. Good quality does not always mean expensive – there are many perfectly serviceable scissors that are inexpensive.

Paper scissors: small and medium sizes are useful.

Fabric scissors: choose a medium or large size, depending on your preference.

Small scissors: used for cutting threads – I have a straight-bladed pair.

Machine embroidery scissors: these have a curved back and short blades. I use these more than any other.

Pinking shears: these have zigzag or scalloped blades.

PINS

Purchase good-quality pins – cheaper types do not have sharp points and can snag your work. Avoid types with plastic heads as these can melt into your work if you catch them with your iron.

Glass-headed pins: the large often colourful heads make these pins easy to see and remove when working.

Glass-headed quilters' pins: these are much longer but ideal when pinning several layers of fabric together.

Long steel dressmakers' pins: optional but useful.

NEEDLES

This is largely a matter of personal choice. Unless it is essential for the technique, I like to use a needle that suits me – rather than one I am told I should use. Find the needle that you are comfortable with in length and thickness.

Embroidery needles: a mixed-length packet is useful. A size 7 is a good general thickness – the higher the number the finer the needle. These have slightly larger eyes so can be used for a variety of threads.

Quilt basting needles: these are much longer needles, medium to fine in thickness, with a large eye. This is my favourite needle to use for every stage of the technique, including quilting. I have found that people who no longer quilt due to problems with their hands have taken up quilting again when using these needles as they give 'something to hold onto'.

Knitters' or wool needles: designed for sewing up knitted garments, these are similar to tapestry needles but much longer. I use them for threading quilting wool into stitched channels; they have a rounded point that will not damage the open-weave fibres (a darning needle is too sharp and a bodkin too blunt to use for this).

Beading needles: these are ultra fine and very sharp – used for attaching beads to fabrics.

IRON

I use both a dry and steam domestic iron depending on what it is needed for. Also it is useful, but not necessary, to have a small travel iron and tiny appliqué iron.

TAPE MEASURE

I have three different types: a small retractable one with both metric and imperial measurements – useful for doublechecking sizes as you sew; a basic good-quality one, around 1.5m (59in) long; and an optional quilters' tape measure – mine is 3m (118in) long. I also have a 30.5cm (12in) long plastic ruler, and 40.5cm (16in) and 45.75cm (18in) square rulers.

STUFFING TOOL

I like to use a cuticle or orange stick; I have found these to be the most useful tools to use for stuffing the filler into the shapes. They are very cheap to buy, and readily available from numerous stores. However, there are several trapunto needles and kits on the market, so work out which you prefer to use.

THIMBLE

There are numerous styles available, in a variety of materials, from silver cups to micropore tape – if it works for you, so be it. Personally, I do not use a thimble – I have tried just about everything but I do not get on with any of them. If my fingers become sore, I use a 'liquid bandage' purchased from the chemist. I paint a couple of layers onto the offending area and replace it as it becomes worn.

SEWING MACHINE

Used mainly for making up items, and with restricted use for the technique, this does not need to be top of the range – it just needs a good basic straight stitch and zigzag stitch.

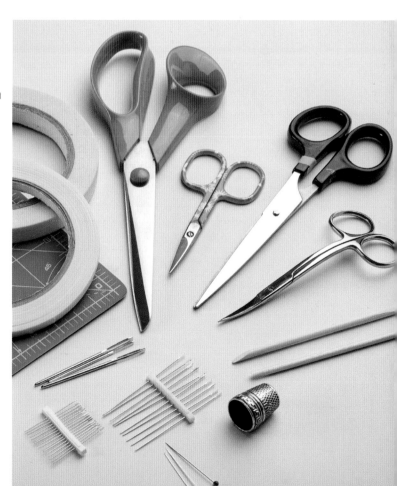

Fabrics

You will be spoilt for choice in the fabrics available to you, but you should abide by certain guidelines if you want your project to be a success: see my 'fabrics to avoid' box, below. When in doubt, always make up a small trial sample first. The fabrics given here will give you the very best results.

Butter muslin (cheesecloth): a fine open-weave material used as the support fabric when creating channels and pockets. It is also used as the final backing fabric for some items, depending on the use and finish required.

Quilters' calico (roclon muslin): this is my particular favourite. It is pre-shrunk with a very even, close weave. It is semi-transparent, allowing your design to be traced directly onto the material, but opaque enough not to let the under layer of stuffing and cording show through on the right side. It is available in both natural and bleached white; bear in mind that heavier calicos will not work in the same way.

Wadding (batting): do not use flat, blanket-type wadding (batting), as it will not allow 'lift' in your work. Preferably purchase it from the bolt, rather than in the pre-packaged plastic bags, as bagged types tend to stretch, distort and wrinkle when unpacked. Select a type that has been treated to prevent bearding – the term used to describe the effect when fibres eventually migrate through to the surface and give a fluffy effect to the finished piece. A few of my favourites include 100 per cent polyester, 2oz (57g) Poly-down. This lightweight wadding (batting) will give your work the 'bounce' it needs for a three-dimensional effect. 100 per cent polyester, 2oz (57g) Thermore wadding (batting) is slightly flatter but still creates 'loft'. I like to use it for table runners and table centres. You could also use silk or wool wadding (batting), depending on the use. Bamboo or recycled plastic products are also available.

Cotton: hand-dyed fine cottons can be used but do not use anything darker than a mid-tone or the dropped shadow effect will be lost on the surface of your work. Subtle mixes of space-dyed cottons can work well if used with careful consideration to the pattern. You do not want your stitching to conflict with the background material.

Silk: use a silk with a smooth surface such as a dupion. This can be a shot fabric (with a different colour for the warp and weft) or a single colour. The colour range is vast and it is easy to work. You must use a support fabric when stitching with silk, such as fine cotton lawn, to prevent the silk fibres being pulled away from the stitching when stuffing and cording.

Tack (baste) this to the back of the silk before adding the butter muslin (cheesecloth). Silk satin can be used if you require a shiny surface for your work – I would advise that you sample it first.

Rayon dupion and satin: smooth rayon dupion can be used, but sample it first to see how it behaves. It might need to be backed with a support fabric. Rayon satin will not be as slippery as silk to handle and will be a little thicker – as ever, trial it first.

Lawn: a very fine cotton fabric that is used as a support material for silk. If it is difficult to find, use a plain white Swiss cotton gentleman's handkerchief instead.

Iron-on adhesive: I tend to use a medium-weight product such as Vilene. This is a non-woven synthetic fabric used as interfacing with heat-activated adhesive on one side. Use it for making quilting templates.

100 per cent polyester toy filling: this will be used to fill the trapunto shapes. If you are making a small item, you can use odds and ends of the 2oz (57g) wadding (batting) for the filling – I am sure we all have bags of off-cuts in our stash! This can be teased out back into its fibrous state and used instead.

Fabrics to avoid

• Avoid fabrics with printed designs and motifs. The work becomes lost in the surface and it is a waste of time to spend all your effort in making a beautiful item that cannot be distinguished on the front of the material.
• Avoid dark fabrics – you lose the drop shadow effect on the surface.
• Avoid furnishing fabrics, woven damask or heavyweight calico as these will prevent the raised pattern from being distinguishable.
• Avoid stripes or fabrics with pronounced slubs in the weave as these will spoil the effect. Also avoid 'novelty' yarns woven into cloth and textured surfaces.
• Avoid 100 per cent synthetic fabrics for the right side of your work.

Threads and yarns

QUILTING WOOL

This is the very best type of yarn to use for cordwork as it is designed specifically for purpose and very versatile. It is spun into a roving that is strong enough to be pulled through channels but as it is loosely spun it can be pulled into very narrow spaces too. If a wide channel requires filling, double it in the needle, and ensure it lays flat as it is pulled into place and does not become twisted. It will cling together and give the impression of a thicker yarn from the right side of the work. It is available in two qualities – as a non-shrunk yarn and also as a pre-shrunk machine washable yarn. It is purchased in skeins.

THREADS

Hand-dyed, space-dyed, variegated or plain. All can be used to create wonderful effects. The main thread that I use is a machine stitching thread. I choose not to use quilting thread as it is too 'springy' for this technique. Any fibre can be used: 100 per cent cotton, a cotton and synthetic mix, 100 per cent polyester or rayon. Metallic threads in single colour or variegated are also fantastic, but I would use those recommended for the sewing machine, as these will not easily shred from the core base when stitching by hand. Stranded embroidery cottons and anything else that takes your fancy can also be used. As ever, try out a sample of the thread if you are unsure of the effect it will create. You may want to avoid very thick threads – it is a personal choice, but I feel these can look clumsy on finished pieces.

BEADING THREAD

This is purchased from bead merchants and craft stores and is specially made for stitching or threading beads. It is semi-transparent, very fine but strong, and is easy to thread into fine beading needles. Available in small reels, there is a more limited colour range than for other threads.

Embellishments

Many of the projects will benefit from having embellishments added at the final stage. These can be purely decorative to add a little sparkle, or functional as fastenings or for quilting. Search around at shows to find the right pieces or visit specialist stores to find what you need.

BEADS

These can be found in numerous sizes, shapes and colours, dull or shiny and every surface in between. Made from plastics, glass or semi-precious stones, they can be purchased individually, in single-colour packs or as themed packs of mixed colours, shapes and sizes. The choice is vast and every price range is covered. They will be sewn in place.

RIBBONS

Silk or double satin-backed ribbons are useful as embellishments or for creating decorative closures. Use in place of zip fasteners.

BUTTONS

These are used as embellishments to enhance a design, or practically for use as closures. Antique or modern buttons can be used – made from metal, plastic, mother-of-pearl, shell, glass, wood or leather. There is a huge variety of shapes and colours to choose from. They are available with two or four holes to stitch in place, or a shank fastening. Self-covered button kits are also useful for matching a button to your project.

DECORATIVE CLIPS

These have various decorative heads and have a split-pin fastening. Found at card-making suppliers.

ADHESIVE JEWELS

These can be made from plastics, semi-precious stones or crystals. They vary in size, shape and price and are purchased individually or in packs. Some are flat-backed, some pointed; jewels with pointed backs have to be fitted into a base and held in place with claws. Some are 'hot-fix', some 'cold-fix' – others are self-adhesive (see page 29).

Stitches

Before embarking on your projects, familiarise yourself with the stitches used throughout the techniques. Many embroidery stitches can be incorporated with the raised work. You can keep to the basic running stitch if you prefer, but I add others to provide definition, variety and texture. Once you are under way and confident, you can vary the stitches as you wish. Add your own interpretation to the techniques – there are no rules!

Basic stitches

RUNNING STITCH

I use this basic stitch to hold together the first two layers of fabric when I start a project. For this stage of the process the ideal stitch size is 2mm ($^1/_{16}$in); the stitches should be no longer than 4mm ($^3/_{16}$in) long or the definition of the pattern will be lost. You can also use running stitch as a decorative or quilting stitch, too. Adjust the size as you like.

TACKING (BASTING) STITCH

This is a variation of running stitch, used to temporarily hold layers of fabric together prior to stitching or quilting. Use large running stitches – between 2.5cm (1in) and 7.5cm (3in) in length – and then carefully remove them when the item is completed. You may want to stitch them in a grid formation, or as single lines, depending on the project.

BACKSTITCH (MY METHOD)

Here I want to share my own method for carrying out this useful stitch; I find it to be a neater and faster way to work than the traditional method. From the front of the work it looks like a solid line of machine stitches but from the back it looks like running stitch. I use it where a solid line is needed to clarify or define areas of the design, or to create added interest. This method is ideal to use as a quilting stitch, too. Start with a knot and bring the needle through to the front at 1. Insert the needle to make a running stitch at 2 and bring the needle up at 3, then go back in at 2. Bring the needle up at 3 for a second time. Repeat these steps again by starting the next running stitch at 4 to continue.

FLY STITCH

This is a decorative stitch that adds texture to work. I add it at the quilting stage and it can sit on the surface of the fabric only – you can quilt with it, but the back of the work will look a bit untidy. Use it to represent small leaf veins, feathers or fern-like structures. Be careful not to make the stitches too large or the threads will catch and may break in domestic use; for this reason it is ideal for use on wall hangings.

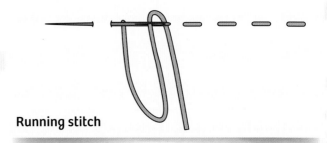

Running stitch

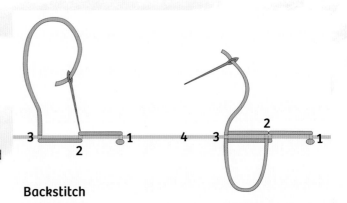

Backstitch

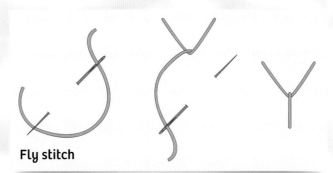

Fly stitch

SEEDING STITCH: SINGLE AND DOUBLE

This is a random decorative stitch – the stitches can be very small and single, up to 5mm (¼in) long, or they can be stitched in pairs, which is known as double seeding. It is best not to stitch in rows or it becomes too formal – unless you want to achieve this effect – instead, stitch in a random way in dense patches ensuring that the stitches keep changing direction. It takes a while to master keeping the stitches all the same size, and can be a slow process, but it is very attractive stitch. It can be used with or without beads for flower centres too. It makes a different background texture if used at the quilting stage, when it is known as stipple quilting, or use it spaced out across the background instead of knotted quilting.

Seeding stitch

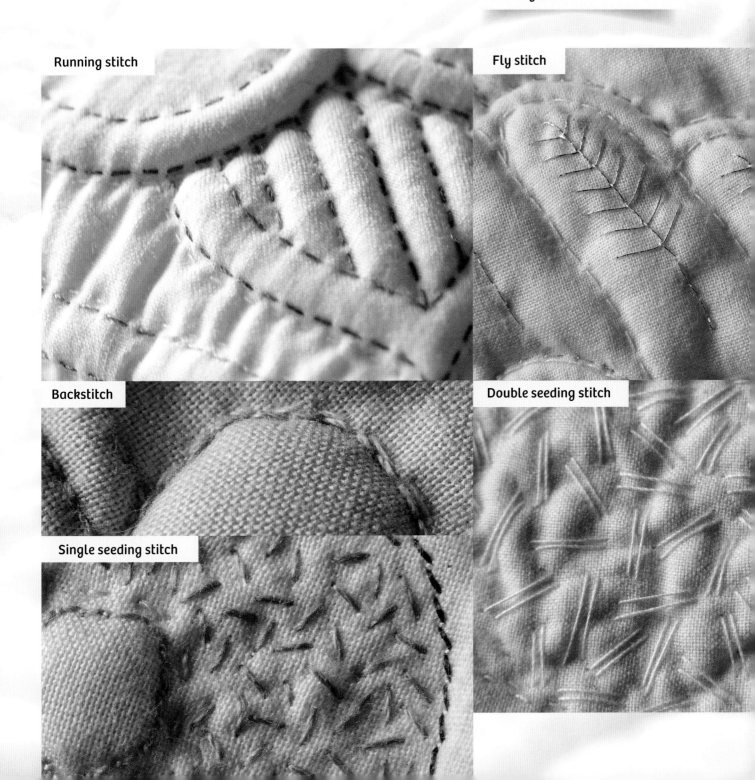

Running stitch

Fly stitch

Backstitch

Double seeding stitch

Single seeding stitch

Further stitches

SATIN STITCH AND PADDED SATIN STITCH

This stitch is used to create a lovely silky, smooth area of stitch. Draw the bead size onto your fabric. Use single fine thread and stitch diagonally across the shape with straight stitches. Fill in the shape. Repeat this in the opposite direction. Finally stitch across the shape on top of the previous stitching in the direction that the bead should be finished. This can be used decoratively for very small shapes.

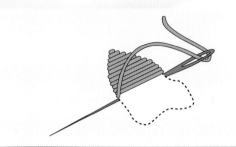

FRENCH KNOTS

These can provide added texture and interest to work or used where beads would not be appropriate. They can be stitched in any type or thickness of thread and they should sit snugly on the surface of the work. For very fine threads, wind the thread several times around the needle or the knot will be pulled through to the back of the work. For thicker threads, wind the thread around the needle once or twice only. When using metallic thread be aware that this is more 'springy' and will make a slightly looser knot. Stitch in clusters or as single knots depending on your design.

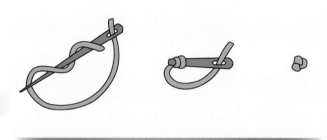

BULLION KNOTS

I use these decoratively where other stitches might not be suitable. They are especially useful to represent small butterfly and caterpillar bodies, the sprig at the top of an acorn seed, or as a textured filling stitch.

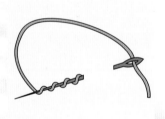

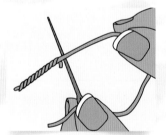

SPLIT STITCH

This is one of the earliest known stitches and was used throughout the Middle Ages. It is found on many sumptuous church embroideries, where it covers the surfaces of fabric and is worked in the finest silk threads. I like to use it for making lines and fine stamens on flower shapes, or for tendrils on plants as an alternative to backstitch. It can be used as a quilting stitch too and has the appearance of tiny chain stitches. It can be worked with a double thread in the needle or a single thread can be split with the needle as it is stitched – from where the name derives.

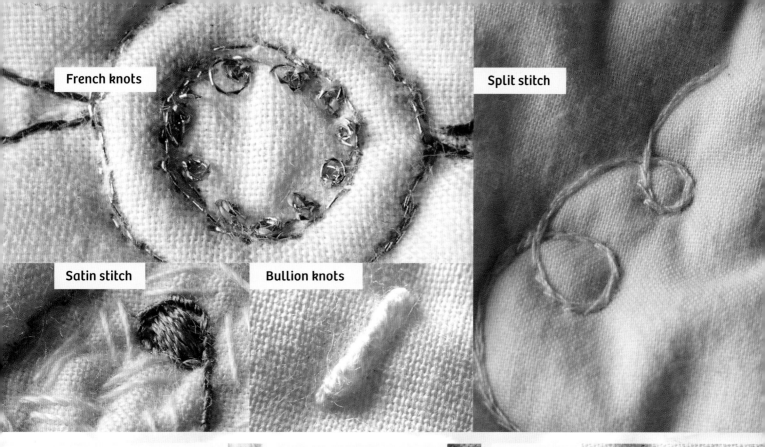

French knots

Split stitch

Satin stitch

Bullion knots

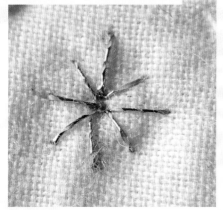

Double cross-stitch star

Double cross-stitch bead

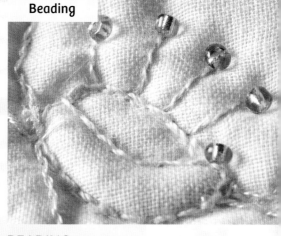

Beading

DOUBLE CROSS-STITCH STAR

This is an ideal stitch to make a star shape. I stitch the vertical and horizontal 'arms' first, making sure that each stitch enters at the centre of the star from the front of the work, then stitch the diagonal 'arms' in the same way. This makes a neater stitch.

DOUBLE CROSS-STITCH BEAD

Use double thread in the needle and make your stitches as small as possible – just under 4mm ($^3/_{16}$in) long. Stitch a vertical and horizontal stitch first, on top of each other, then stitch the diagonal stitches across the top, also the same size. This will make a neat raised 'bump' on the top of your work, or it will sink into the surface when used as an alternative to knotted quilting. Try this in various thicknesses of threads with a dull or shiny finish.

BEADING

This term is used to describe attaching beads to fabric. These can be sewn on individually or in clusters. It is advisable to use a beading needle, which is long and very fine, enabling the thread to be passed through the hole in the bead. These can be stitched to the surface in a variety of ways depending on the desired effect. It is a good idea to sew the beads in place with a strong thread made for this purpose. If beading thread is not available, try running your sewing thread through beeswax to strengthen it and help prevent it becoming tangled or knotted. Secure the beads firmly to the fabric and use a matching colour to stitch with where possible.

Further stitches

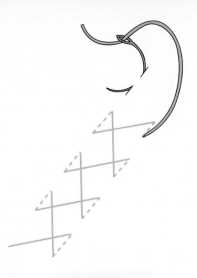

HERRINGBONE STITCH

This is a useful closure stitch. If you have accidentally cut too many threads in the butter muslin (cheesecloth) when making a hole at the back of a trapunto shape, the fabric will need to be closed to prevent the stuffing from working its way out. As the fabric is an open weave it will easily distort the shape if the edges are pulled together too tightly. Stitch across the hole from side to side without pulling the fabric too close together.

LADDER STITCH

This stitch is used for invisible closures on items such as pincushions and pillows; once the pincushion is filled with stuffing, or a pad is placed inside a pillow, the opening that is left needs to closed as discreetly as possible. The ideal stitch length should be 2mm ($1/16$in). This stitch is also useful for stitching linings in place. It sits flat and is far less bulky than over-sewing stitches.

LAIDWORK

This is a decorative textured stitch that sits on the surface of the work. It is perfect for adding decoration to padded areas such as acorn cups, thistle heads or just to add interest to a design. The base threads are laid over the shape – this can be horizontally and vertically or diagonally – and then held in place with a second thread, where the base threads cross over. The holding thread can be a small straight stitch or a cross-stitch and it can be in a contrasting colour or thickness to the base threads. The stitch is found in many Elizabethan embroideries.

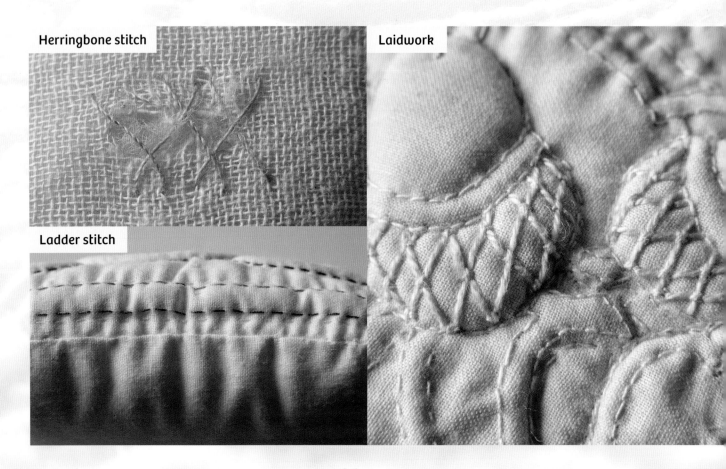

Herringbone stitch

Ladder stitch

Laidwork

Quilting stitches

ENGLISH QUILTING

A quilt is made from a sandwich of three layers of fabric: the top, the interlining and the back. All are held together securely by stitching – this is known as English quilting. Take a matching thread. Make a knot at the end of it. Put your needle somewhere into the top of the sandwich and bring it out where you want to start quilting, pulling it through so that the knot embeds in the interlining. Start quilting using a running stitch through all the layers of the sandwich. If you prefer, make one stitch at a time or stab stitch from top to back and back to top. To finish, make a backstitch and run the thread into the layers. The start and the finish are unseen. Make sure the stitches are even and that every stitch comes through to the back. The thickness of the sandwich will determine the size of the stitch – they will get smaller and neater with experience. Quilting is usually stitched in a diagonal cross-hatch design or in parallel lines.

MEANDER QUILTING

Draw a continuous line that travels across the area to be quilted in a 'loopy' style. Practise your line on paper first so that it is visually pleasing. Make your quilt sandwich and proceed as for English quilting. Use my version of backstitch for this quilting if the areas to be filled are small.

KNOTTED QUILTING

This is a simple form of quilting that can be very decorative. Mark a series of dots regularly or irregularly with an HB pencil on the top surface of the fabric. Using any strong thread, take a stitch through all layers of the sandwich on one of your marked dots. Take another stitch in the same spot. Pull both ends of the thread and tie a reef knot – a type of double knot. Cut the ends of the thread, leaving no less than 5mm (¼in) in length. The ends are traditionally left on the quilt top. A variety of threads may be used: try coloured knitting yarns, embroidery threads, metallic threads, or different threads together. Ensure that the thread used, once knotted, will not undo.

BUTTONING

This is similar to knotted quilting. Fasten the threads in the same way, but leave the cut ends on the back of the work, or sew the button on in the usual way through all of the fabrics, then hide the ends between the layers.

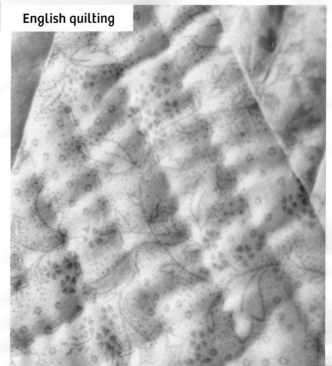

English quilting

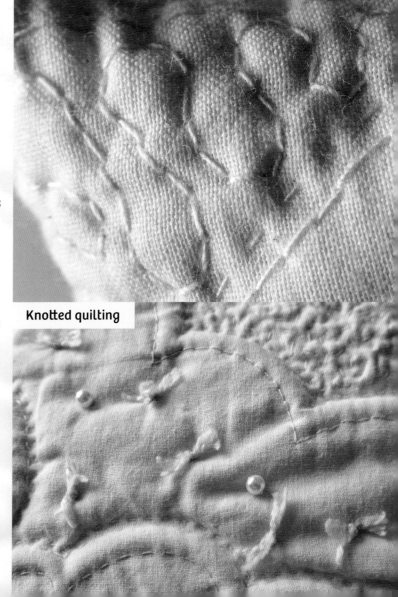

Meander quilting

Knotted quilting

WHIPPED QUILTING

Stitch with English quilting, then with a second thread oversew through each quilting stitch without picking up the fabric below – it creates a continuous line. This type of quilting can be stitched with self or contrasting colours. This is a useful technique to use with problem threads that are difficult to pull through the fabric layers. It may be used at the initial stitching stages too.

STIPPLE QUILTING

When seeding stitch (see page 23) is used for quilting, it is referred to as 'stipple'. A variety of textured finishes can be achieved depending on the scale and closeness of the stitch. I like to use it in background areas in place of cross-hatching – when viewed from a distance the random stitches in self colour create an effect that is similar to rough-cast plastering. It is a slower process than other forms of quilting.

STITCH IN THE DITCH

This term is used to describe the quilting stitch worked in the seam-line where two fabrics have been joined together in patchwork. It can also refer to quilting between two stitched areas for the raised work.

Machine stitching

Although I have used a sewing machine to make up some of the finished items, I rarely use machine stitches for the traditional raised quilting – they can sometimes be used alongside hand quilting but I have found that too many problems occur to make it worthwhile pursuing. Because of this, most of my designs are not suitable for machine stitching. I personally feel that the point of using traditional techniques is to create a hand-worked item that removes the need for stitching solely by machine.

If it is imperative to stitch by machine, you will need to use a medium to small stitch length for the best results and be very accurate with your machining otherwise the end result will be far from attractive. Unless your machine is your 'third hand' do not attempt to use coloured thread but keep to colours that perfectly match the background fabric. This way any slight inaccuracy will be hidden in the finished product.

Common machine pitfalls

Here are a few common pitfalls to be aware of if you do want to sew with a machine:
- Many machines do not stitch well on the single thickness of fine calico (muslin) even when it has the open-weave material on the back.
- A 5mm (¼in) foot would need to be used when stitching the double parallel lines and these can be difficult to achieve when stitching across the bias on the fabric as it can distort the overall shape.
- You cannot use a twin needle as this will create problems when trying to thread the wool into the channels.
- You cannot use the reverse stitch when you stop and start stitching as this shows and looks unattractive on the right side of the fabric – instead, at the start and finish of each stitched line you will need to take the upper thread through to the back and knot them together to prevent them from coming undone.
- Stitching multiple lines can become tedious and labour-intensive. However, if you remove the feed dogs and free-stitch the design, it may not be easy to control and mistakes are very difficult to rectify.
- At the quilting stage, it is difficult to machine the surface of the work, as it is very uneven and in many places will not allow enough room for the work to go under the needle.

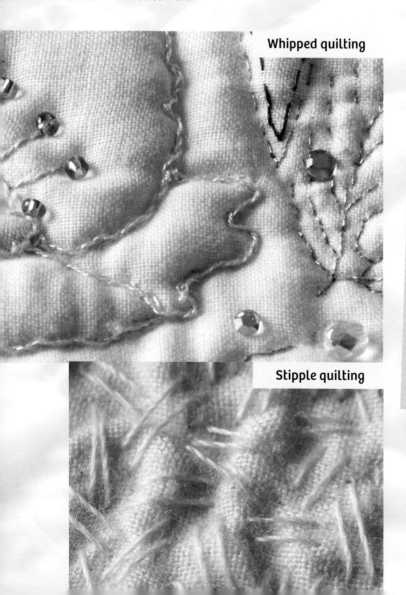

Whipped quilting

Stipple quilting

Attaching embellishments

The term 'embellishment' refers to a way of adding decoration to the surface of fabric, but can also be used to describe visible fastenings – buttons and beads are included under this umbrella. Here I will go into detail on attaching gemstones and crystals or other decorative items that cannot be stitched in place.

ADHESIVE JEWELS

'Hot-fix' jewels are flat-backed and do not have any holes to allow them to be stitched in place. A domestic or travel iron may be used to attach them, but make sure you cover the gemstone with a silicon sheet or baking parchment to protect both the iron and the stone. Place the flat back of the stone onto the fabric and carefully put the iron on top of the protective covering, then apply the stated temperature, time and enough pressure to melt the adhesive, which will stick the stone in place. Leave to cool and the glue will cure and fix the stone in place permanently. Follow the supplier's instructions and always do a trial first.

The alternative is to use an embellishment tool made for the sole purpose of fixing stones in place. It is similar to a large pen that is heated like an iron, and comes with various attachments depending on the size of the stone to be fixed. It is heated to the correct temperature by electricity, so take extra caution when using it, as the application tip becomes extremely hot. There is an adhesive on the back of the jewel that melts when heat is applied. Place the stone onto the fabric and place the tip of the tool, upright, on top of the stone. This melts the glue in the same way as the iron – the glue cures as it cools and is not easily removed. By using this tool you have more control for positioning the stones and it is a faster method. It is worth investing if you intend to embellish vast areas. The most expensive Swarovski and Chinese crystals are fixed this way.

'Cold-fix' crystals and gems are flat-backed and non-stick. Purchase the recommended glue for fixing the stones to fabric. Place a small quantity of glue to the flat back with a cocktail stick, and use tweezers to manipulate the jewel into place – apply a little pressure to ensure it has stuck to the fabric. You can add the glue directly to the fabric if you prefer but this is a bit fiddly. Allow twenty-four hours for the drying process to complete. These stones are not easily removed when cured. They are also highly reflective and available in the same range as the hot-fix stones. Most are washable when fixed.

SELF-ADHESIVE STONES

These simulate the above but are made from plastics. They are normally used in creative card-making, but will sometimes stick to fabrics. They can be a bit hit and miss – I have had various results: some are excellent and stay in place virtually permanently for years, while others fall off easily! If you like these and wish to use them, cold fix into place to ensure they will stay on the fabric, but do not allow an iron or hot fix tool near them or they will melt.

Creating the three-dimensional quilting

So is my work trapunto? Only in part... Trapunto is a word that I now hear over and over again and it has somehow become the go-to term to describe all raised work. This is the reason why I call my work 'corded and stuffed' – it encompasses all of the techniques that are put together to become the raised quilting.

To understand how my patterns work and to be familiar with the combined techniques, I suggest that you start here, work through the steps and make the pincushion. Every stage is fully explained and this will be your reference throughout the rest of the projects. The 'Dog Rose' design used to make the pincushion is stitched with colour, so, from the back of the work, you will easily see the areas that have to be stuffed and corded.

The basic execution for all the projects in this book is identical, only the designs, shapes, colours and sizes change to make each one different. Other relative information will be explained as necessary for each project. Read everything carefully before you begin each project and re-visit this chapter whenever you need to.

▶ 1

Instead of toy filler, you can use off-cuts of polyester wadding (batting), which will need to be shredded into fibres.

Using the design

For each project I have broken down the design process into two or three stages, to make it as clear as possible. In this case I have used three stages. The first stage is the basic pattern that you will need to transfer onto the fabric. The second is a stitching guide and illustrates which areas will require additional stitching before you can cord and stuff. The third is the final stage when you quilt through all the layers and the additional dimension to the finished piece is revealed. Each project follows the same basic stages.

Template 1

Make this your initial tape placement.

Template 2

Template 3

TEMPLATE STAGE 1

This is the design for the pincushion. It shows only the basic shape that you need to transfer onto your fabric using a sharpened HB pencil, or propelling pencil. For every project, this initial design stage is also given at full size on the pull-out templates at the back of the book.

TEMPLATE STAGE 2

The areas that need to be stuffed (using trapunto) are marked on the design in pink. Additional lines of stitching for the 'multi-channels' of French-style cording are marked with green dashed lines. The channels that need to be threaded (referred to as cording) with quilting wool (Italian quilting) are coloured green.

TEMPLATE STAGE 3

The final stage has red dashed lines to indicate which areas are selectively quilted to achieve the illusion of the layered effect. In some of the more complex projects, the embellishments are also indicated on Template 3.

Transferring the design

Take one of the fabric squares and fold it diagonally from corner to corner. Lightly press, then open out. Secure your Template 1 design to a flat surface with a few pieces of masking tape to prevent it from slipping. I also find putting a couple of sheets of white paper under the design before I start very useful, as it helps the design show through more clearly. Place the fabric onto the design, aligning the diagonal folds with the pattern and secure with masking tape as before. Lightly trace the design onto the fabric with the pencil, being careful not to make the image too dark (2). Draw all the lines that you see including the one around the outer edge of the design. This will be the right side of the work.

▶ 2

Start tracing at the top of the design and work to the bottom – this will prevent the pencil smudging onto the fabric if your hand is covering the work.

You should be able to see your design through the fabric, making it easy to copy. If this is not possible, you will have to use a lightbox; if you don't have a lightbox, place a light underneath a glass table and tape your designs to the surface as an alternative.

Layering and tacking (basting)

Remove the paper design. Take one of the squares of butter muslin (cheesecloth) and place it on the back of the front fabric. Using your tacking (basting) thread, fasten the two fabrics together with a tacking (basting) stitch that is just under 2cm (¾in) long (3). Start at a top corner and work diagonally across the fabric to the opposite bottom corner. Repeat for the other corner, then tack (baste) the fabrics together all around the square about 1cm (½in) inside the raw edges.

Butter muslin (cheesecloth) is placed on the back of the design.

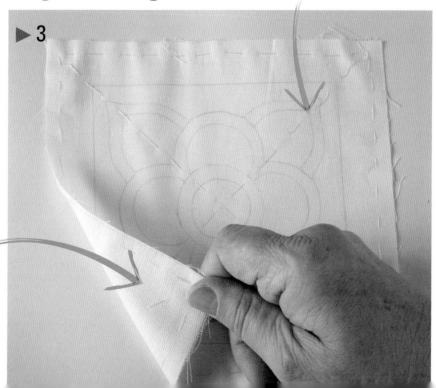

The diagonal tacking (basting) stitch that holds the two fabric layers together.

▶ 3

Stitching the outlines

Start with the yellow thread; do not use a length longer than 30cm (12in), as it can easily become twisted and knotted as you work. Make a good-sized knot at the end of the thread and, with the knot on the back of the work, begin by stitching the inner circle with a small, neat, even running stitch on the drawn lines through both layers of fabric (4). When the circle is complete, take the thread to the back and fasten off with a few backstitches in the butter muslin (cheesecloth). Cut off the thread and repeat for the second circle in the centre of the design. You will have two parallel circular lines in yellow.

Change to the cerise thread, start in the same way and stitch the inner half circles, which are the petals. You do not need to fasten off for each petal – you can take your thread across the back and come back up at the beginning of the next petal.

Fasten off when all four are stitched. You will find that as you stitch on the pencil lines, providing they are not too dark, they should begin to disappear.

Stitch the outer petals with the cerise colour – this is a continuous line – and make a backstitch to form a 'V' shape where the petals meet. This will create a nice sharp design and give you two parallel lines. These double channels of stitching will later be threaded with wool for Italian quilting.

Change to the green thread (mine is variegated) and stitch the first inner leaf shape. Take your thread under and stitch the outer shape. Fasten off. Repeat on all four leaves. Fasten off the thread. Use yellow thread to stitch the square outline, backstitching at the corners. Press the work on both sides.

▶ 4

Use a long needle so that you can put several stitches on the needle at one time.

The completed initial stitching.

Stitching tip

Always start in the centre of the design and work out to the edges – this prevents a 'bubble' of fabric appearing on the surface of the work if the materials shift in the stitching process. This is very important when working on large items and quilts where the backing fabrics can become wrinkled.

Stitching the additional lines

If you look at the stitched pincushion (see bottom right and pages 40–41), you will see that there are additional lines of stitching that do not appear on the first template; these lines are indicated on Template 2, but should not be drawn on with pencil. Instead, I use 5mm (¼in) wide masking tape as a guide to ensure that these extra lines are straight and all the same width. When working over large areas, the tape can also help stabilise the fabric and prevent it stretching, when stitching on the bias.

The leaf shapes all contain additional lines. Cut a piece of masking tape longer than the area to be stitched and place it on the fabric where indicated on Template 2, page 32. It is important to put the first tape in the correct position so that subsequent rows will be even. The tape makes good straight channels and eliminates the need for measuring and drawing onto the fabric. Thread your needle with green thread and start with a knot at one end of the tape. Sew with running stitch along the edge of the tape as close as possible without allowing the needle to pierce the tape – if it does, it will become sticky and make the stitches very difficult to work. Stitch to the end of the line within the shape, take the thread to the back of the work and come up on the other side of the tape to continue stitching (5).

When both sides of the tape are stitched, there is no need to fasten off. Leave the needle on the wrong side of the work ready to sew the next line, remove the tape from the work, then re-place it, butting it up close to one side of the previous stitching (6). Stitch along the edge of the tape. Remove the tape and repeat the process until half of the inner leaf shape is filled with lines. Fasten off. Complete the remaining half of the shape in the same way.

Repeat the stitching on all four leaves to give you multiple rows of running stitch – these will become the channels for the French-style cording. Apply tape all around the outside of the yellow stitched square to form an outer channel. Change to cerise thread and sew running stitch around the edge, remembering to sew a backstitch at the corners. Do not worry if the back of the work looks untidy – it will later be covered and no one will ever see it. Press the work again to give a smooth flat finish to the fabric – it will not be possible to press the fabric beyond this point.

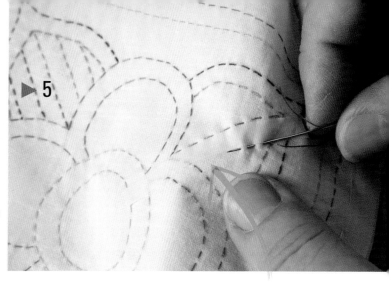

▶ 5

The tape is in position and the stitching almost complete.

▶ 6

The first channel is stitched.

Place the tape alongside the first parallel rows of stitching.

The leaf now has the parallel lines of stitching within the inner shape and the outer shape is completed too.

Masking tape tips
Always remove masking tape from your fabric once you've finished a stitching session. Otherwise, the adhesive can sink into the surface of your fabric and leave a permanent stain. This might not happen overnight, but it is good practice to ensure you remove the strips each time.

Stuffing

Carefully remove the diagonal tacking (basting) stitches only from the work. The centre of the flower motif has become a circular pocket and is now ready to be stuffed with a little toy filler – this is called trapunto work. See Template 2, page 32.

Turn the work to the wrong side; you will be working from the back of the design for the next two stages. Take the fabric in your hand and push the pointed end of the stuffing stick into the middle of the motif pocket, being careful not to push the stuffing stick through to the front of the calico (muslin) fabric (7). Pull apart the open-weave threads of the butter muslin (cheesecloth) and make a hole by waggling the stick from side to side. You can be reasonably forceful when doing this as the hole will need to be slightly larger than 5mm (¼in) in diameter to allow you to fill it easily.

Keep the work in your hand. Tease out a little of the toy filler and carefully ease it into the hole (8). Use the flatter end of the stuffing stick to do this. Push in a little at a time to fill the pocket, keeping the filler flat and soft. Do not be tempted to twist it into the space with the stick as the filler will just go into small ball shapes and will make a very bumpy, ugly shape that will not flatten. The secret of trapunto is not to over fill the pocket as this causes the fabric that surrounds it to pucker and distort. There should be sufficient filler to allow the shape, when viewed from the right side, to be raised up from the background and form a little shadow across the fabric.

Once the pocket is filled, if the hole you have made is very big, carefully push the open-weave threads back together with the stuffing stick (9). When using the technique, frequently look at the right side of the work to check the result. Look to see if there is either too much or too little filler in any pockets that have been filled and adjust accordingly.

► 7

Tease apart the fabric's fibres using your stuffing tool. The back of the work looks untidy as the ends of the threads and knots have been well secured in the butter muslin (cheesecloth).

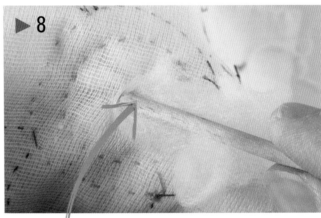

► 8

Gently push the filler into the circular centre.

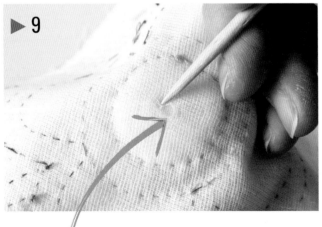

► 9

Pull the open-weave threads back together if the hole becomes very large to prevent the filler from working its way out of the shape.

The right side of the work showing the raised trapunto centre. This is how all raised areas should look – without any puckering on the surrounding fabric.

Cording

Continue to work from the back, using Template 2, page 32, for reference. Take the large-eyed, blunt-ended needle and thread it with a length of quilting wool about 50cm (20in) long. It is best to use this length as a maximum, unless otherwise stated. Begin with the channel created by your first two yellow lines. Using the needle, part the loose fibres of the muslin (cheesecloth) fabric and thread the needle into the channel. Ease it a quarter of the way around the circle. Bring the needle out of the channel and pull the wool through far enough to leave a 1cm (½in) tail projecting from the starting point.

Thread the wool back into the channel, in through the same hole, and continue threading for another quarter of the circle (10). As you pull the wool back into the channel, leave a small loop at the re-entry hole – this will allow for any shrinkage of the wool during laundering; if you are using a pre-shrunk wool, as I did, you can pull the wool right through. Continue in the same way until the circle is complete. Exit from the channel at the point of entry and cut off the wool leaving another 1cm (½in) tail (11). The quilting wool does not need fastening off.

From this point onwards I worked the photographs out of order so that the techniques would be as clear as possible. Follow the stages given in the text and refer to the finished threaded piece on page 38 if need be.

Next thread the cerise petal channels. Start threading the wool at the channel close to the previous circle leaving a 1cm (½in) tail. Follow the shape round and exit halfway around the first petal. Leave a loop when re-entering and continue threading up towards the inner circle. Remove the needle, pull the thread through and when re-entering the channel leave a loop. Continue in this way for the remaining three petals leaving loops as before until the channel is complete. Finish by leaving a tail and cut off the wool. If you are using pre-shrunk wool, only leave loops where the next petal is joined (close to the inner circle), so that the wool stays in position on the design. If the wool needs joining, only do this where you would make a loop close to the inner circle.

Now start on the leaf shapes (12). First thread the outer shape and leave a loop at the pointed end of the leaf. Next thread each of the straight channels in the inner leaf shape individually, leaving tails at either end. If the channels at either edge of the inner shape are narrow, it is still possible to thread these with the quilting wool, as they will look odd if left empty. Finally thread the outer square leaving loops along the edge if applicable or only at each corner if using pre-shrunk wool.

Key cording tips

As a guide, leave small loops of wool about every 7.5cm (3in) on long straight, curved or circular shapes. When using pre-shrunk wool you need only leave loops on corners, tops of pointed shapes and at the bottom of inverted points or if changing direction along a channel. Tails are left at the beginnings and ends of straight lines, and at ends of shapes if needing to join the wool. The same wool can be used in very narrow channels and doubled in the needle if the channels are wide.

▶ **10**

The needle is returned to the channel via the exit hole.

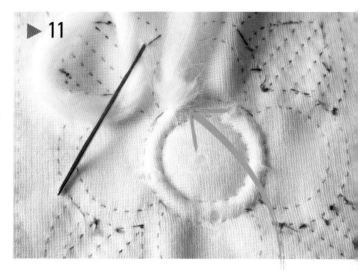

▶ **11**

The circle is complete and the wool exits at the entry point ready to be cut off. The example here does not have shrinkage loops, as the wool was pre-shrunk – you can see the entry and exit holes around the circle.

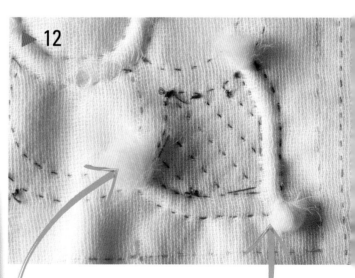

12

This is the length of tail that is left at either end of the outer leaf channel.

This is the size of the loop that should be left at the re-entry point.

The back of the work will look like this when all the cording is complete. The wool is left like this as it does not need to be fastened off.

The front of the work will look like this when complete. Traditionally it would have been finished at this stage and would have had a fabric added to cover the back.

Adding wadding (batting)

▶ 13

Give the work a gentle tug in all directions to ensure all the channels are filled and the work is squared up. You could finish it here – all the techniques are complete in their own right, but I take it a stage further. I add another layer to make the design into a three-dimensional technique. Put the square of wadding (batting) to the back of the work and place the remaining square of butter muslin (cheesecloth) behind the wadding (batting) to make a quilt sandwich (13). Tack (baste) the layers together as before.

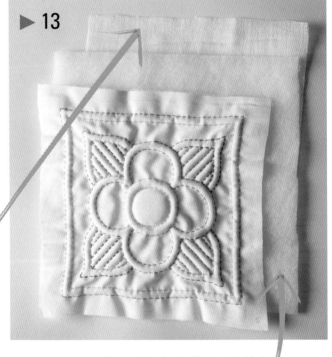

Butter muslin (cheesecloth) is the backing fabric for the pincushion.

The wadding (batting) is placed behind the stitched design.

38

Final quilting

Complete the final quilting with sewing thread that matches your background material so that the stitches are almost invisible – here I am using white. Refer to Template 3, page 32, to see which areas will be selectively quilted to enhance the design. Knot the end of your thread and begin quilting the inside of the centre circle just alongside the yellow stitches, but not on top of them. Your quilting stitches may not be the same size as the running stitch, as the wadding (batting) has now been added and this will make it difficult to match the size. You do not have to hide the knots at the back of the work as this will not be seen.

Next, quilt around the outside of the circle close to the second row of yellow stitches (14). You will see that the quilting has emphasised the trapunto and it looks as if it has additional stuffing inside. The first channel of cording is now more pronounced. Now quilt around the outside only of the petal shapes. As you quilt across the leaf shape, you should stitch close to the cerise colour – this will be referred to as stitch in the ditch quilting, where you have to quilt between two previously stitched shapes. As the petal shapes were not stuffed, you will now see that by quilting outside of the petal cording, they look as if they are filled and give the impression that the flower shape is raised above the leaves. Quilt around the outside only of each leaf shape, close to the green stitching. This will appear to raise the leaves away from the background. Finally quilt just inside the yellow square and then outside the pink corded outline square. Add masking tape around the outer edge of this square and butt it up to the last row of quilting. Quilt around the outside edge of the tape through all the layers with the white thread. This will be the seam-line and act as the guide when making up the pincushion.

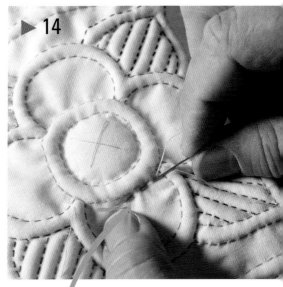
▶ 14

The inner circle is quilted and the outer circle is in progress.

Making up

The extra white fabric square is for the back of the pincushion. Place the pincushion right side down onto the fabric square and carefully pin and tack (baste) along the quilted seam-line, around three sides of the pincushion. Machine stitch on this line, remembering to leave the fourth side open. Double stitch the corners to reinforce them. Trim away any excess fabric to leave about 5mm (¼in) and neaten using a zigzag stitch on the sewing machine, or by over-sewing by hand. Clip across the corners to reduce bulk and carefully turn through to the right side.

Use closed scissors to carefully push the corners out into a good shape. Stuff the pincushion firmly; fill to bursting with toy filler – it will resemble a ball shape. Turn in the seam allowance, pin in place and close with ladder stitch. Flatten the pincushion by clapping it between your hands several times. This will give you a good shape and expel any excess air from the filling (15).

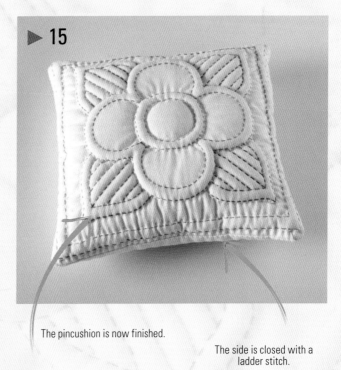
▶ 15

The pincushion is now finished.

The side is closed with a ladder stitch.

The flower motif appears to be made up of several layers, each stitched to the background – this is an optical illusion made by the final quilting, which is hardly visible. Be careful when stuffing your pincushion, as if the filling is not adequate the pins will not be held in place.

Adapt the colours as you wish to suit your own style. You could even just use one thread colour for a monochrome finish.

The projects

The following pages contain nine projects to whet your appetite, each containing a simple but very effective combination of techniques carried out in a traditional way. Each project follows the same basic construction – the only real difference is the overall design and the use of stitches. The pincushion project (see pages 30–41) has all the information that you will need in detail – if you have followed the stages and made it for yourself, the projects will hopefully fall into place. We begin with the easiest and build up to the more intricate designs.

All the template stages are given within each project, and all the basic outline templates are also given at full size on the book's pull-out sheet. To obtain the best results, please read all the instructions carefully before starting each project and refer back to previous pages for other information if you need to. Always start each stage at the centre of the design and work towards the outside edge unless otherwise stated. Please note that throughout I have used the term 'stuff' to refer to the trapunto areas with each design, and 'cord' to refer to threading the wool for the Italian quilting and French-style corded areas.

Moon Flower needlecase

▶ 14 x 14cm (5½ x 5½in) FOLDED

I love the late-summer Japanese moon flower plant, so I made this the starting point for the front of the needlecase. I have stylised the flower and tried to retain its fresh open character. I have used a pale-coloured background fabric and stitched the motif in a contrasting variegated single colour thread. It is quilted in a colour to match the background fabric. The lining matches the colour used for the stitching of the design.

Three-dimensional quilting

You will need

- One 30 x 19cm (12 x 7½in) piece of plain cotton fabric (or quilters' calico/muslin – I used green)
- Two 30 x 19cm (12 x 7½in) pieces of butter muslin (cheesecloth)
- One 30 x 19cm (12 x 7½in) piece of Thermore wadding (batting) – as an alternative, use 2oz (57g) polyester wadding (batting) and carefully steam press it between two pieces of cotton calico (muslin) to achieve the same flatter effect. You will not need to have additional interfacing, as this is quite firm
- One 28 x 17cm (11 x 6½in) piece of fabric for the lining (I used bright blue)
- One 23cm (9in) square piece of felt for the needlecase pages
- 60cm (23¾in) very narrow satin ribbon to colour match the lining fabric
- Two small buttons
- Small quantity of toy filler (or scraps of teased-out polyester wadding/batting)
- Skein of quilting wool
- Sewing machine thread for stitching the design (I used blue)
- Sewing machine thread for quilting (I colour matched the fabric)
- 5mm (¼in) wide, low-tack masking tape
- 30 x 19cm (12 x 7½in) piece of tracing paper
- HB pencil

Template 1, see also full-size pull-out template

1 When using coloured material, copy the design onto tracing paper with a pencil or use a lightbox to transfer your design. Then trace it onto your fabric. Tack (baste) one piece of butter muslin (cheesecloth) to the back of the fabric in grid formation, as this is a larger design than the pincushion project and will need more tacking (basting). Stitch the flower motif with running stitches for the two centre circles. Stitch all the flower petals with backstitch, and the inner framework of the needlecase. Stitch the outer flower shape with running stitch. Do not stitch the six lines that radiate out from the flower centre yet.

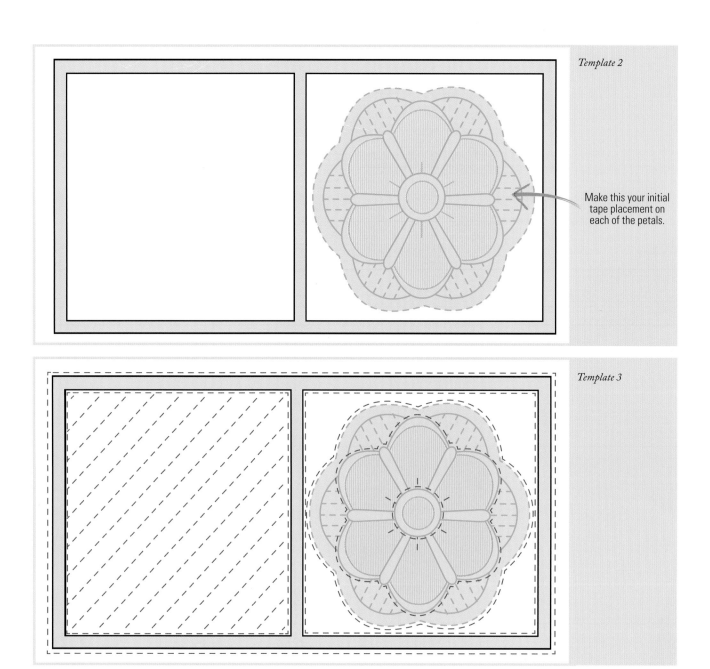

Template 2

Make this your initial
tape placement on
each of the petals.

Template 3

2 Using Template 2 for reference, stitch all the masking tape lines with running stitch. Start with the outer flower shape, then stitch the parallel rows within the petals. Remove all the tacking (basting) stitches. Press both sides of the work.

3 Turn the work to the back. Stuff the centre of the flower and each petal. Using the quilting wool, cord the circle that surrounds the centre of the flower. Cord the narrow shapes between the petals, also the curves at the ends of the petals and cut the wool leaving a tail at each end of the channels. Cord the outer flower shape leaving small loops in the dip between each curve. Cord the parallel rows and cut the wool at the end of each channel, leaving a tail. Finally, cord the centre spine of the needlecase and all around the outside edge, leaving a small loop of wool at each corner.

4 Add the wadding (batting) and the second layer of butter muslin (cheesecloth) to the back of the work and tack (baste) all the layers together.

5 For quilting guidance, see Template 3. Change to the thread that matches the background fabric. Start with the flower motif, then, when completed, quilt around the inner edge of the front and back of the needlecase, then the outside edge. Finally, quilt the diagonal lines on the back by using two strips of 5mm (¼in) masking tape placed side by side to make 1cm (½in) spaces. Change back to the original thread colour and stitch the straight lines that radiate out from the flower centre, as single big stitches to form indentations on the petals. Remove the tacking (basting). With the original colour thread and a small running stitch, sew a row of stitches through all the layers 3mm (¹⁄₈in) away from the quilting around the outside edge of the needlecase. Ensure that you can see these stitches on the wrong side of the work.

Making up

1 You will see that the quilting has pulled the work in a little on the front of the needlecase, but this will not show when it is made up. Trim the work to 28 x 17cm (11 x 6½in), to match the size of the lining fabric.

2 Place the right side of the work onto the right side of the lining. Pin the fabrics together and tack (baste) around the outside edge, just outside the last row of stitches that you should now clearly see on the wrong side.

3 With the wrong side of the work uppermost, machine stitch all the fabrics together just inside of the last row of stitches – do not sew into the quilting line! Leave an opening of 5cm (2in) along the narrow back edge of the work so that it can easily be turned through. Trim away any excess fabric so that it leaves 5mm (¼in) seam allowance all around. Carefully trim across the corners to reduce the bulk and turn the work to the right side. Push out the corners carefully. Pin, then close the opening with ladder stitch.

4 Press around the outer edges of the work on the lining side, using a medium heat and a dry pressing cloth. Tack (baste) through all the layers at the centre of the needlecase, either side of the spine.

5 Cut the square of felt in half to make two 23 x 11.5cm (9 x 4½in) rectangles. At this stage it is optional to trim around the edges with pinking shears (or a pinking rotary cutter) if you have them, to make a decorative finish.

6 Place one rectangle of felt on top of the other and pin and tack (baste) together through the centres to make the 'book'. Lay the felt book onto the needlecase – lining side up – and pin in place along the spine – check it folds to close properly.

7 Attach the pages by stitching either side of the centre line into the wadding (batting), with two rows of small running stitches. Ensure that these stitches do not go through to the right side of the work. Remove all tacking (basting).

8 Cut the ribbon into two equal lengths. Fold each piece in half and attach the fold to the lining just inside the centre front. Neaten by stitching a button over the fold. Repeat with the other ribbon at the centre back edge. Fold closed and tie the ribbons into a bow.

The open needlecase shows the 'pages' stitched in place and the ribbon fastenings neatened with small buttons.

The ribbons are tied together to form a double bow.

▷ Variations

It is very easy to create a matching needlework set from the pattern. The pincushion uses the same design and it is set on a 17cm (6½in) square of fabric. The scissor keeper is made from a 20cm (8in) square of fabric, cut in half diagonally, to make the triangle. Half the pattern is drawn onto the triangle, setting it 1cm (½in) away from the long edge. I have added another petal shape to the centre of the design to fill the point of the triangle.

48

The final quilting almost disappears when using the same colour thread as the background fabric.

► Variations

Intertwined initials are quilted into the back of the pink silk dupion needlecase with metallic thread. In this example I swapped the ribbons for a decorative button with a thread loop closure. The threads to make the closure are self wrapped (whipped) to strengthen the loop. See also page 120.

49

In a Twist bucket bag

▶ 28 x 25cm (11 x 10in)

During the early 1950s, the 'bucket bag' became a very popular shopping accessory. The name described the shape of the bag, usually made from a variety of coloured plastics with steel rivets to hold the handle in place (attached from the front to the back) and to decorate the top and bottom edges of the bag. It had an oval base to create a more stylish look and was designed to hold plenty of shopping. I clearly remember my mother and aunts each having these bags in cherry red, black and white. I decided to make my own version – not to be used as a shopping bag, but large enough to hold all the essentials for an evening out. I have given my bag some shaping to make it more interesting, attached the handle from side to side, added covered buttons for closing and shaped pearl buttons for embellishment. The front and back are alike, so work each stage together.

You will need

For the body of the bag:
- Two 36 x 36cm (14 x 14in) pieces of quilters' calico (muslin) for the front and back of the bag
- Four 36 x 36cm (14 x 14in) pieces of butter muslin (cheesecloth)
- Two 36 x 36cm (14 x 14in) pieces of 2oz (57g) polyester wadding (batting)
- Two 30.5 x 28cm (12 x 11in) pieces of fabric for the lining

For the base (optional):
- One 23 x 15cm (9 x 6in) piece of quilters' calico (muslin)
- Two 23 x 15cm (9 x 6in) pieces of butter muslin (cheesecloth)
- One 23 x 15cm (9 x 6in) piece of wadding (batting)
- One 19 x 14cm (7½ x 5½in) piece of lining fabric

For the handle:
- One 56 x 6cm (22 x 2½in) piece of quilters' calico (muslin)
- One 56 x 4cm (22 x 1¾in) piece of wadding (batting)
- One 56 x 5cm (22 x 2in) piece of lining fabric

- One skein of quilting wool
- Small amount of toy filler (or scraps of teased-out polyester wadding/batting)
- Sewing thread to match the colour of the bag
- Tacking (basting) thread in pale blue, green or pink
- Two 2cm (¾in) self-covered buttons
- Scraps of bag fabric and wadding (batting) for covering the buttons
- Six 2cm (¾in) decorative flat buttons
- 5mm (¼in) wide, low-tack masking tape
- Needles
- Stuffing tool
- HB pencil

The covered button with a rouleau loop closure. The matching button on the other half of the bag is a decorative feature.

Three-dimensional quilting

Template 1, see also full-size pull-out template

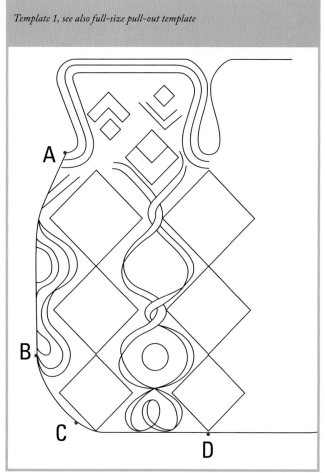

Template 2

1 The template here gives half the bag – the bag is symmetrical, so you will need to draw out the entire shape using Template 1: mirror image one half and align the centre point (D) on both pieces. Place the design underneath a 36cm (14in) square of quilters' calico (muslin), leaving an equal amount of fabric all the way around the pattern. Secure both the design and the fabric to a flat surface and lightly trace the design onto the fabric using the pencil. Include the balance marks A–D for matching the front and back when making up later. Remove the paper template. Tack (baste) one piece of butter muslin (cheesecloth) to the back of the fabric with a 2.5cm (1in) grid and add a final tacking (basting) to the outer edge of the design 1cm (½in) away from the raw edges of the fabrics. Repeat this for the second piece of quilters' calico (muslin).

2 For this design, I have backstitched all the small shapes and all the twisted patterns to make them distinctive – especially the narrow channels that twist across each other. The remaining diamond shapes and the bag's upper outlines are stitched with running stitch. Stitch all the basic lines that have been drawn onto the fabric for both the back and the front.

3 Use Template 2 as reference to add all the extra lines of stitching where indicated, using the masking tape to create the channels. Start from the outside edges of the diamonds and work towards the centre. Sew with running stitch. You can carefully bend the tape around the curved shapes at

the top edge of the bag. Repeat on your second piece of fabric. Remove all the tacking (basting) from the bag pieces leaving only those that are on the outside edge of the fabric.

4 Turn the work to the back and stuff all the pink areas shown on Template 2. Be careful not to over-stuff each shape. Repeat with the second piece. Next add the cording; if you have to join the wool, only do so at the corners of a shape or at any 'V' shape that might appear within a design. Start with the twisting channels – you will be able to use the wool as it is for the very narrow channels because it does not have a tight twist when spun so it will easily fit. Start at the bottom edge of the bag and work up to the top. Thread each channel separately, leaving a tail each time you exit and enter the spaces. Do not tug the wool when threading, but ease it into each channel taking care not to pull it up into gathers. Next thread the concentric squares that make the diamond shapes: start with the channels closest to the centre of the shape, work to the outside leaving a loop on each corner and thread each diamond channel separately. Next thread the half shapes at the top edge of the bag: use double wool in the wide channels. Finally, cut a longer length of wool – approximately 66cm (26in) – and thread this into the upper shaped edge, easing it carefully through the inner channel first. Do not let it gather along the top and corners. Finish with the outside channel. Then complete the second half of the bag in the same way.

5 Pin and tack (baste) both halves to the wadding (batting) and butter muslin (cheesecloth) with a grid.

6 Use Template 2 to complete the quilting. Start in the middle of the bag shape and quilt from top to bottom, working towards the outside edge. Use the same thread that you used to stitch the design. Finally, quilt around the top shaped edge either side of the channels. Repeat the quilting on the other half of the bag. Change to your coloured tacking (basting) thread and stitch with very small tacking (basting), through all the layers: sew 5mm (¼in) away from the top edge of the design and 3mm (⅛in) away from the side seams and bottom edge.

7 For the base of the bag use the templates given below: trace the design onto the fabric, remove the paper template, then tack (baste) one piece of butter muslin (cheesecloth) to the back. Use running stitch to sew the main design. Add the masking tape to make the extra channels as shown on bag base, Template 2. Remove the tacking (basting) stitches, leaving the outside line in place. The base does not have any trapunto stuffing, so from the back, thread all the diamond shapes as before and double the wool for the shaped edges, then finish with single wool for the outside edge. Add the wadding (batting) and butter muslin (cheesecloth), tack (baste) together and quilt where indicated, working from the centre to the outside. Remove the tacking (basting) stitches and stitch around the outside edge 3mm (⅛in) away from the final quilting.

A detail showing a backstitched, twisted shape with the pearl button embellishment, running stitch diamonds and final quilting that creates the additional raised three-dimensional effect for the design.

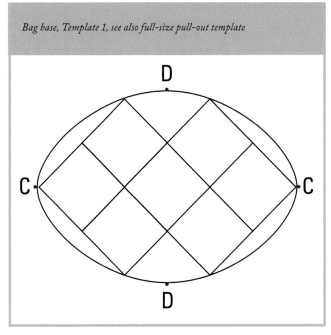

Bag base, Template 1, see also full-size pull-out template

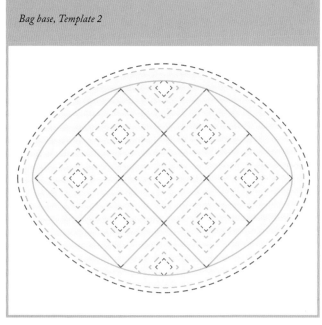

Bag base, Template 2

53

Making up

1 Add a 1cm (½in) seam allowance beyond the template line. Repeat for the base. With running stitches – about 5mm (¼in) long – sew through all the layers on the pattern line. Do this for each half of the bag, to keep the fabrics in place. Cut out each half of the bag along the seam allowance lines. Cut out the base, 1cm (½in) beyond your last corded channel.

2 Using one half of the bag as a pattern, cut out the lining the same size as the bag and transfer the balance markings to the lining. Repeat for the other side of the bag. Cut out the base lining using the bag base as the pattern. Put to one side.

3 Remove the tacking (basting) and running stitch along the top edge of the bag to point A, then carefully trim away the butter muslin (cheesecloth) and wadding (batting) close to the line of quilting. Fold the calico (muslin) seam allowance over to the back of the bag along the quilted line, pin in place and with a small herringbone stitch sew this to the wrong side of the bag just into the wadding (batting). Gather the calico (muslin) to fit around the top convex curve and cut small notches into it to allow it to stretch around the concave curve towards the side seams then pin and stitch in place. (If you do not wish to add a base into your bag, see the tip box below right for construction advice.)

4 Remove the running stitch from the sides and bottom edge of the bag and the base shape, then trim away the butter muslin (cheesecloth) and wadding (batting) close to the small tacking (basting) in the coloured thread. With right sides together, match both the pattern and the balance points on one side of the bag and pin. Tack (baste) then machine with a medium-length stitch from point B to point C inside the coloured tacking (basting) line along the seam-line. Look at the right side of the work to see if you have matched the seam correctly. If necessary make any adjustments then stitch the other side from point B to point C.

5 Setting the base shape into the bag is done in two stages. First ease the base into the bottom of the bag, then match the balance points on one half of the base to the bag from point C to point D to point C. Pin, tack (baste) and stitch together. Complete the other half of the base in the same way. Make a second row of stitching 3mm (⅛in) away from the first row, then trim the seam allowance to 5mm (¼in).

6 Complete the side seams by matching the pattern, then pinning, tacking (basting) and stitching from point B to point A on both sides of the bag, with a 1cm (½in) seam allowance. Sew a second line of stitching as before, making a double stitch to reinforce the opening at point A. Turn the bag to the right side and check that the pattern matches correctly. Make up the lining in the same way but do not turn it through.

7 Sew the button embellishments to the front, side and back of the bag. Use flat, two- or four-hole buttons only so that they do not protrude too far but indent into the surface.

8 With leftover calico (muslin) cut an 11 x 2cm (4½ x ¾in) strip of fabric on the bias. Fold in half, right sides facing in, along the length and machine stitch the strip together to make a tube with a 5mm (¼in) seam allowance. Carefully turn this through to the right side to make a rouleau strip. Press. Fold in half to make a loop. Stitch this securely 1cm (½in) down to the inside of the bag at the centre back top edge.

9 Put the lining into the bag, matching up the side seams, and pin in place with the seams opened flat. Continue to pin the lining to the top of the bag – it should protrude by 1cm (½in). Trim it level with the top edge and around to the side seams. If there is any excess lining fabric, make a small pleat at each side seam.

10 Fold the lining to the inside along the top edge of the bag, about 5mm (¼in) from the edge. Pin and tack (baste) in place. The bag will look neater if the lining is 3mm (⅛in) away from the curved top edge and down to the side seams. Sew the lining to the bag with a small ladder stitch or slip stitch.

11 Next, the handle. With right sides together, pin and stitch the lining and calico (muslin) together on the long edge with a 5mm (¼in) seam. Starting from the same end as before, stitch the other long sides together with a 5mm (¼in) seam. As the lining is narrower than the calico (muslin), stitching from the same ends will prevent the fabric from twisting. Turn the strip through to the right side and press flat so that the lining fabric has an equal amount of the calico (muslin) visible on each side to look like binding. This will be the right side. Thread the wadding (batting) through the handle to pad the strip, being careful to keep it flat. Re-press lightly. Sew with a small running stitch along each open end 5mm (¼in) from the edge. Fold each end to the right side along the stitched line, then fold either side in so that the ends of the handle become 2cm (¾in) wide; tack (baste) together.

12 Stitch the handles securely to the inside of the bag at the curved opening, 2cm (¾in) down from the side seam. Ladder stitch in place.

13 Cover two buttons with scraps of calico (muslin) following the maker's instructions. I always add a small circle of wadding (batting) to the top of the button before covering as it gives a better finish. Stitch a button to both the centre back and centre front of the top edges of the bag. Close with the rouleau loop.

Alternative bag shape

If you are not adding a base, join the front to the back of the bag from point B to point C to point D to point C to point B first, and check the pattern matches. Then join the sides from point B to point A. Add the second row of stitching by sewing from point A right around to point A. Repeat with the lining.

You could add a plain base and cross-hatch quilt it if you do not want to cord and stuff it. You will need to add a stiffener to the base if you want to keep it plain or else it will not retain its shape.

The top edge of the bag. The lining is ladder stitched in place and the handle is fastened inside at the side seam.

◀ Variations

A small evening bag, measuring 18 x 16.5cm (7 x 6½in).

The design can easily be made in a smaller size. This version is made from quilters' calico (muslin) with the initial stitching carried out in black; all the quilting is stitched with a gold thread. The bag is made in two halves without the base. The top edge has a single channel sewn with backstitch along its upper edge. It is lined with a black fabric that is printed with a broken ice design in gold. I have used two antique black and gold buttons for the rouleau loop closure.

55

Out of India pillow

▶ 43 x 43cm (17 x 17in)

Paisley motifs are intricate, abstract, curved teardrop shapes, derived from the palmette motif of Persian rugs – the design can be traced back over 2,000 years. This pillow was created as a companion piece to my 'Symphony 2000' quilt (see pages 124–125), and was based on a small rough sketch taken from the paisley centre. Once I decided on the finished size for the item, I scaled up the initial sketch and refined it until I was happy with the outcome – the refinement process is usually influenced by the size and shapes within the design and whether it will be practical to carry out the techniques. For this pillow, I added the knotted and beaded embellishment and the single stipple quilting.

Three-dimensional quilting

Template 1, see also full-size pull-out template

You will need

- Two 50cm (20in) squares of quilters' calico (muslin) for the front and back of the pillow
- Two 50cm (20in) squares of butter muslin (cheesecloth)
- One 50cm (20in) square of 2oz (57g) polyester wadding (batting)
- One skein of quilting wool
- Small amount of toy filler (or scraps of teased-out polyester wadding/batting)
- Sewing thread to match the colour of the pillow
- Tacking (basting) thread in pale blue, green or pink
- 5mm (¼in) wide reel of low-tack masking tape
- Skein of twisted embroidery thread, or fine crochet thread to match the pillow fabric
- 43cm (17in) pillow pad
- Needles
- Stuffing tool
- HB pencil
- Thirty 2mm (¹/₁₆in) pearl beads
- Beading needle

1 Take one 50cm (20in) square of calico (muslin). Put one piece aside. Secure the design to a flat surface and place the calico (muslin) directly on top of the design leaving an equal amount of fabric all the way around the pattern. Secure the fabric to the flat surface and lightly trace the design from Template 1 onto the fabric using the pencil. Tack (baste) one piece of butter muslin (cheesecloth) to the back of the calico (muslin) with a 2.5cm (1in) grid and add a final row of tacking (basting) to the outer edge of the design 1cm (½in) away from the perimeter edges of the pillow pattern.

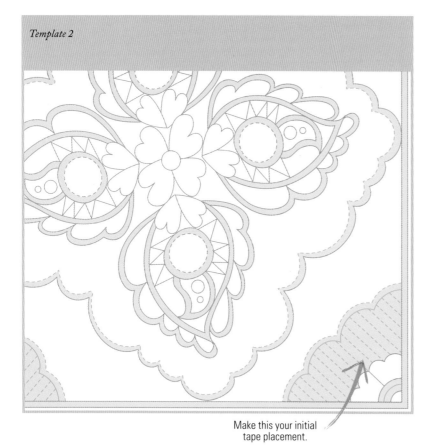

Template 2

Make this your initial tape placement.

Template 3

2 Refer back to Template 1. For this design, I have backstitched all the small shapes within the paisley motifs, the heart shapes and the heart-shaped centre, the corner shapes, the inside edge of the large scalloped shape that surrounds the paisley design, plus the inside edge on the scalloped corners. The remaining areas are stitched with the basic running stitch. Stitch all the basic lines that have been drawn onto the fabric.

3 Use Template 2 to add all the extra lines where indicated using the masking tape to create the parallel 5mm (¼in) channels. Sew with running stitch. You can carefully bend the tape around the curved shapes where necessary. Remove all the tacking (basting) from the work, leaving only the tacked (basted) border on the outside edge of the pattern. Carefully press both sides of the work.

4 Turn the work to the back and stuff all the pink areas shown on Template 3. Be careful not to over-stuff – especially the very small shapes within the paisleys. Do not forget to stuff the corner shapes.

5 To cord, refer back to Template 2. Start with the channels surrounding the stuffed centre of the paisley shape. Do not tug the wool when threading, but ease it into each channel. Continue and complete the motif, remembering to leave very small loops where the design changes direction. For soft curves, only leave a loop at the bottom of each if the curves are continuous or form a row. Thread the continuous large scalloped shape that surrounds the central design. For the corners, thread the scallop shape first, then thread the parallel channels separately, leaving a tail each time you exit and enter each one.

6 Thread the outside channel that surrounds the design. This will give the pillow a sharp, square finish so you will not have to make any piping cord when making up the item. If you are careful, you can use a longer piece of wool, but no more than 1m (39½in). Leave a loop at each corner – and a tail if you need to re-join the wool. If you are using a pre-shrunk wool, only leave loops at the corners to keep the corner square – if you are using non-shrink wool, you have to leave loops along the about every 7.5cm (3in) to allow for shrinkage.

7 Pin and tack (baste) the wadding (batting) and butter muslin (cheesecloth) to the back of the pillow and tack (baste) all the layers together in a grid formation. Then tack (baste) around the outside edge as before.

8 Refer to Template 3 when quilting – you need only quilt selected areas now, as this will create a more sculptural effect. Start in the middle of the pillow and, with the basic quilting stitch, work from the centre towards the outside edge. Use the same thread that you used to stitch the design. Stipple quilt with a small single stitch in the areas indicated with pink dots at the centre of the quilting guide. Then stipple quilt the background areas indicated with pink dots. This is a slower form of quilting but very effective. You could quilt this area with a 1cm (½in) cross-hatch pattern if you prefer. The orange stars indicate the places to add the tied quilting. Test out the knot with the thread you have chosen (use the area with the extra fabric that surrounds the pillow) to see if it stays tied. Double the thread in your needle and take the needle through all the layers to the back of the work leaving a 2cm (¾in) tail on the right side of the work. Bring the needle back up to the front about 2mm (¹/₁₆in) away and tie a tight double knot. Cut off the thread leaving the same length tail. Tie all the knots where indicated. Also add four knots to the quilted centre where the heart shapes join together. If the knots work loose but you like the thread you are using, you will have to make a small stitch through each knot with your sewing thread to keep them securely tied.

9 Embellish with beads at each of the blue dots marked on Template 3. Stitch these securely through all the layers using the beading needle.

10 Change to your coloured tacking (basting) thread and stitch with very small tacking (basting), through all the layers, 3mm (¹/₈in) away, all around the outside edge of the final quilting on the pillow.

Making up

1 The second piece of calico (muslin) will be used for the back of the pillow. Place your quilted pillow front right side down onto the pillow back and carefully pin and tack (baste) along the coloured guideline tacking (basting), slightly stretching the front to match the back fabric for all four sides of the pillow.

2 Machine stitch on this line, leaving an opening of about 20cm (8in) along one side to allow the work to be turned back through. Double stitch the corners to reinforce them. Trim away all the excess fabric to leave about 5mm (¼in) allowance outside the machine stitching line, and neaten by using a zigzag stitch on the sewing machine, or by over-sewing by hand.

3 Clip across the corners to reduce bulk and carefully turn through to the right side. Use closed scissors to carefully push the corners out into a good shape. Insert the pillow pad through the opening. If the pillow looks too flat, try inserting a slightly larger pad, or use a feather-filled pad, which is slightly heavier than a polyester fibre pad. Pin and tack (baste) the opening closed, then sew with a ladder stitch. Trim all the tails on the knots to be 5mm (¼in) long.

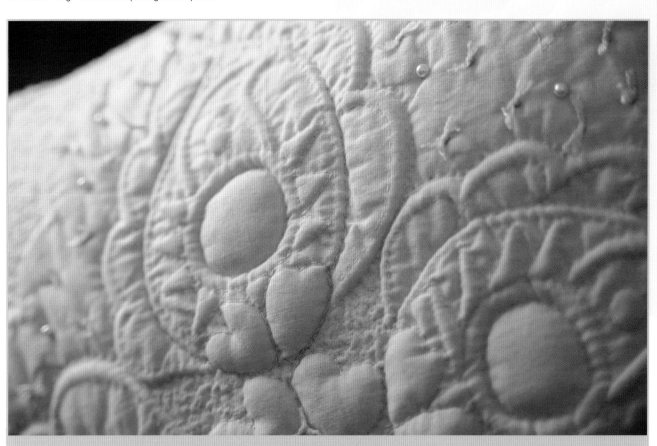

Paisley motifs – detail showing the stuffed and quilted areas.

Here you can see the beaded and knotted quilting.

The background shows the small single stipple quilting. The stitches can be either 3mm (⅛in) or 5mm (¼in) in length: here they are 3mm (⅛in) throughout.

60

The centre of the pillow shows the stippled quilting and tied knots. The final quilting emphasises the sculptural effect, giving the impression of multiple layers on the surface of the pillow. The pearl beads add a touch of luxury to the textured surface and contrast with the matt finish of the calico (muslin).

Blue Dahlia quilt

▶ 138 x 138cm (54½ x 54½in)

In the past, several people have told me that they love the idea of making a three-dimensional quilt using the raised techniques but that the idea of embarking on a whole cloth design was somewhat daunting. With this in mind I designed a quilt that combined patchwork blocks with raised stitched centres – this gives the best of both worlds as it can be made as a scrap quilt or as a quilt with each block made from the same fabrics. Although this project is a nine-patch quilt, by adding extra blocks – or omitting some – you can make it any size you wish.

Dahlias come in a wide variety of sizes, shapes and colours and I have always loved their big blowsy blooms; I can clearly remember when I was a child that most of the front gardens in our village were full of dahlias in the Autumn. I would marvel at the tiny ball-shaped bud that would become a magnificent multi-petalled flowerhead. This became the starting point for the centre of each block. I have kept the raised centre quite simple, then chose to introduce two surrounding colour-ways (Blocks 1 and 2) to make the quilt more interesting. The centres are all identical and they are stitched with coloured threads that reflect the colours in the fabrics. The quilting pattern in the border reflects the centre of the raised motif and I have added a thin border and binding to the quilt made from the same colour as the inner petals of the flower, which contrasts with the overall colour scheme. The button embellishment represents the buds. It is a good idea to make up one block from spare fabric before starting so you can familiarise yourself with the construction.

You will need

All sizes are based on a 112cm (44in) fabric width unless otherwise stated

For the raised centres of the nine blocks
- 1.5m (1¾ yds) quilters' calico (muslin) for the blocks and border
- 81.5cm (32in) of butter muslin (cheesecloth) 1m (39in) wide
- Ivory-coloured machine sewing thread
- Machine sewing threads to stitch the centres in colours to match your fabrics

To surround the raised centres and create five 'Block 1' squares:
- 1.5m (1¾ yds) fabric for Template B (this includes the border fabric)
- 50cm (20in) fabric for Template C
- 50cm (20in) fabric for Template D
- 25cm (10in) fabric for Template E (this also includes enough for the 'Block 2' squares)

To surround the raised centres and create four 'Block 2' squares:
- 50cm (20in) fabric for Template B
- 50cm (20in) fabric for Template C
- 50cm (20in) fabric for Template D

- 1.5m (1¾ yds) fabric – to contrast with Blocks 1 and 2 for narrow border and binding: I chose peach to match the inner petals on the flower
- 1.5m (1¾ yds) darker colour fabric for the border that frames the blocks: I used turquoise
- 1.5m (1¾ yds) backing fabric, 1.5m (1¾ yds) wide, or use leftover fabrics, which can be pieced together
- 154 x 154cm (60 x 60in) of 2oz (57g) polyester wadding (batting): Polydown cut from the bolt is the best
- Two skeins of quilting wool
- Bag of toy filler (or scraps of teased-out polyester wadding/batting)
- Two reels of matching sewing thread for stitching the quilt together
- Tacking (basting) thread in a pale colour so that it shows up against the printed fabrics
- 5mm (¼in) reel of low-tack masking tape
- 1cm (½in) reel of low-tack masking tape
- A small amount of medium-weight iron-on interfacing for making quilting templates
- **Optional:** fifty-four flat pearl buttons 1cm (½in) wide to embellish (do not use shank buttons as these will stand away from the quilt when sewn in place)

Preparing your blocks

Each of the nine blocks in the quilt is made up in the following way: each has an identical raised embroidery centre (A), and then colourful patches are attached around them to create five 'Block 1' patches, which feature lighter fabrics, and four 'Block 2' patches, which feature darker fabrics. Cut the fabric as follows to create all the necessary pieces. The templates are given on the pull-out template sheet at the back.

▶ BLOCK 1 (LIGHTER FABRICS, MAKE FIVE)

- **For Template B:** eight strips 4cm (1½in) wide and 1.5m (1¾ yds) long from this fabric and put to one side to use later for the border

  Ten 17cm (6½in) squares – then cut these across diagonally to make twenty triangles

- **For Template C:** ten 15.5cm (6in) squares – then cut across diagonally to make twenty triangles

- **For Template D:** ten strips 5cm (2in) wide from across the width of the fabric; use the template and cut these into twenty pairs

- **For Template E:** nine 10cm (4in) squares – then cut across diagonally to make eighteen triangles

▶ BLOCK 2 (DARKER FABRICS, MAKE FOUR)

- **For Template B:** eight 17cm (6½in) squares – then cut across diagonally to make sixteen triangles

- **For Template C:** eight 15.5cm (6in) squares – then cut across diagonally to make sixteen triangles

- **For Template D:** eight strips 5cm (2in) wide from across the width of the fabric; use the template and cut these into sixteen pairs

- **For Template E:** nine 10cm (4in) squares – then cut across diagonally to make eighteen triangles

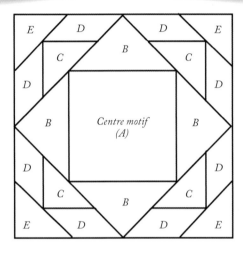

Three-dimensional quilting

Template A: 1, see also full-size pull-out template

Template A: 2

Make this your initial tape placement.

▶ FOR THE NINE RAISED BLOCKS

1 Cut four strips 6cm (2½in) wide and 1.5m (1¾ yds) long from the quilters' calico (muslin) and put to one side to use later for the border. Cut nine 26.5 x 26.5cm (10½ x 10½in) squares from the quilters' calico (muslin). Cut nine 26.5 x 26.5cm (10½ x 10½in) squares from the butter muslin (cheesecloth).

2 Draw a 20cm (8in) square in each of the calico (muslin) fabrics, leaving an equal amount of material all around the edge. Secure the design to a flat surface. Put the calico (muslin) directly on top of the design so that the drawn square lines up with Template A: 1. Secure the fabric to the flat surface and lightly trace the design onto the fabric with the pencil.

3 Remove the template. Pin, then tack (baste) one piece of butter muslin (cheesecloth) to the back of the marked fabric with a 2.5cm (1in) grid and add a final row of tacking (basting) along the outer edge of the drawn square.

4 Next stitch the main design – always work from the centre towards the outside edge. Running stitch is used throughout. Do not stitch the six small circles that surround the flower motif unless you are going to stuff them – these indicate the position of the buttons. Do not stitch the short lines that radiate from each petal near the centre of the flower.

5 Use Template A: 2 and add the extra stitching lines where indicated. Use masking tape to create the 5mm (¼in) channels. Remove all the tacking (basting) stitches from the work, leaving only those that are on the outside edge of the pattern. Press both sides. Repeat for all nine blocks.

6 You will now need to use your thirty-six triangles cut using Template B. The darker fabric triangles must be applied to four stitched centres; the lighter fabric triangles must be applied to five stitched centres. Fold under by 5mm (¼in) the long edge of each triangle. Stitch to one side of a stitched central square, matching the fold to the drawn line. Trim the calico (muslin) to the same seam allowance as the fabric. Repeat, adding the next triangle to the opposite side of the stitched centre. Press away from the centre. Finally add the last two triangles to the stitched centre in the same way. Do this for all nine blocks.

7 To stuff the centres, turn the work over to the back and stuff only the pink areas shown on Template 2. Be careful not to over-stuff each of the shapes as you don't want to distort the fabric surface. Repeat for the other eight blocks.

8 To cord, start in the centre of the design and thread the circle. Thread the pointed petals and leave small loops where the shape changes direction. Next thread the outer channel on the half-circle shape, then thread each of the parallel channels separately. Start and finish the cording with a tail approximately 5mm (¼in) long. Repeat for the other eight blocks.

9 Check that all the blocks are all the same size – they should measure approximately 29cm (11½in) square.

Template A: 3

Detail, Block 1, showing the raised quilted centre of the block complete with button embellishments.

65

Creating the patchwork

1 Use a 5mm (¼in) seam allowance throughout unless otherwise stated. Make up your Block 1 squares. Pin, tack (baste), then stitch one pair of Template D parallelograms to either short side of a Template C triangle (refer to the diagram on page 64). Trim the shorter side if necessary so that the strip measures 10cm (4in) wide. Press away from Template C. Add a Template E triangle to make the corner of the block. Press the seam allowance towards the corner. It is important to press at every stage. Repeat this process for the remaining fabrics for Block 1 – check that the twenty Block 1 triangles are the same size.

2 Pin, tack (baste), and stitch the triangles created in step 1 to the corners of each of the five Block 1 raised centres. Stitch the opposite corners first, as before. This will give you five completed blocks – each measuring approximately 40cm (16in) square.

3 Repeat steps 1 and 2 to create the sixteen Block 2 triangles, and to stitch them to the corners of the four Block 2 centres. Trim all the blocks, if necessary, to the same size.

4 Set the blocks out in a three-by-three square, alternating Blocks 1 and 2 – use the photograph right, for guidance. Pin them to a sheet or design wall, so that during construction the blocks remain in the correct order. Sew the blocks together to form three alternating horizontal strips.

5 Carefully match Rows 1 and 2 together, with right sides facing, then pin and tack (baste) them together. Stitch, then remove the tacking (basting) stitches and press the seams open. Join Row 3 to Row 2 in the same way. Press as before. Stitch a small tacking (basting) line all around the four sides of the quilt along the seam allowance. Mark the halfway point on the seam allowance on each side.

Creating the borders

1 Measure the quilt sides – they should be approximately 117cm (46in). Cut four 2.5cm (1in) by 119cm (47in) strips from the 11.5m (12¾ yds) length of contrast fabric. Mark the half-way point on the long edge of each strip, on the right side of the fabric. Fold each one in half widthwise, with wrong sides together, press. Open out and pin one strip, along the crease line, to the quilt seam allowance matching the halfway points. Stitch this to the side of the quilt on the crease line. Fold the contrast fabric back together, pin and stitch through the layers, on the right side of the fabric 5mm (¼in) below the fold. Take time to be accurate. Repeat on the opposite side of the quilt, then on the two remaining sides (top and bottom).

2 Cut four 2.5cm (1in) by 119cm (47in) strips from the 1.5m (1¾ yds) length of darker fabric. Mark half way along the length as before. With right sides together, pin one of the darker strips to the contrast fabric – match the halfway points and stitch to the contrast fabric just above the 5mm (¼in) seam allowance to cover the previous row of stitches. Press towards the outside of the quilt edge. Repeat on the opposite side as before, then the remaining two sides (top and bottom).

3 Next, the mitred border. With the pre-cut strips of calico (muslin) and Template B fabric, make four borders by stitching one Template B strip to either side of a calico (muslin) strip. Press the seams away from the calico (muslin).

4 Fold each border in half lengthwise and mark the centre with a pin. Find the centre of each side of the quilt top and mark in the same way. Start with the sides of the quilt: with right sides together, matching the centres, line up the sides of the quilt and pin. The borders should equally overlap the sides at each end. Stitch using a 5mm (¼in) seam allowance starting and stopping 5cm (2in) from each end of the quilt top. Fold out and press towards the edge. Repeat with the top and bottom borders.

5 Fold back the overlapping corners to create mitres. Ladder stitch the mitre together from the front of the work, through all the layers. Turn to the back, machine stitch along the ladder-stitched seam and cut away excess fabric to leave a 1cm (½in) seam allowance. Thumb press the seam open and press flat. Complete the stitching to each corner of the quilt to finish the border.

6 To create the final border, re-measure the quilt sides – they should now be approximately 134cm (53in) long. Cut two 3 x 134cm (1¼ x 53in) strips from the darker fabric. Stitch to one side of the quilt – press towards the outside edge. Repeat on the opposite side.

7 Cut two more strips from the darker fabric: 3 x 140cm (1¼ x 55in). Stitch these to the two remaining sides (top and bottom). The quilt should now measure about 140cm (55in) square. If you are not using a whole piece, make up a piece of backing fabric measuring 150cm (60in) square from the leftover fabrics.

Detail, Block 2, shows the very narrow border that gives a flash of contrasting colour, which matches the stitching in the centre of the block.

Top row, left to right, Blocks 1–2–1.

Middle row, left to right, Blocks 2–1–2.

Bottom row, left to right, Blocks 1–2–1.

Making up the quilt

1 Place the backing fabric, right side up, onto the wadding (batting) and tack (baste) together with very large stitches in a star shape. Turn the fabric over so that the wadding (batting) is uppermost and place the quilt on top with an equal amount of excess fabric showing all the way around. Tack (baste) the three layers together in a 7.5cm (3in) grid format – periodically check that the backing fabric remains smooth while you are stitching.

2 Start quilting with the centre block. With ivory-coloured thread, stitch in the ditch around the raised block, then follow Template A: 3 (page 65) to quilt the flower motif.

3 To quilt Template B, start at the outer edge of the triangle and stitch in the ditch round the four sides of the square. Echo quilt Template B using the 1cm (½in) masking tape as a guide. Quilt from the outside edges of the template and work towards the centre.

3 To quilt Template C, stitch in the ditch on its outside edges then echo quilt 1.5cm (²/₃in) apart, working towards the centre of the block.

4 To quilt Template D, stitch in the ditch along the outside edge of the block. To quilt Template E, stitch in the ditch along the edge that aligns with Template D.

5 Quilt each of the nine blocks in the same way.

6 Stitch in the ditch along the quilt edge where the blocks meet the borders. Stitch in the ditch where the darker fabric meets the Template B fabric, along either side of the calico (muslin) strips, then where it meets the final border.

7 Sew with a small running stitch through all the layers 1cm (½in) away from where the last border is joined to the quilt. This should leave 5mm (¼in) of border remaining. This is the edge of the quilt. Trim the excess wadding (batting) and backing fabric to this edge. Measure the quilt through the centre, both ways – this will give the finished size as the quilting will have pulled the fabrics in a little – it is should now be approximately 138cm (54½in) square.

8 The next stage is to bind the quilt. From the bright contrast fabric cut two 3 x 137cm (1¼ x 54in) strips. Start with the sides of the quilt. With right sides together, pin the raw edges of the first strip matching it to the edge of the quilt and sew 5mm (¼in) from the edge through all layers by machine with a medium-length stitch.

9 Fold the binding strip over to the back of the quilt, so that the binding sits flat, and covers the raw edges of the quilt. Fold under the raw edge of the binding until it touches the previous row of stitching. Hand-stitch this folded edge to the back of the quilt with either a hemming stitch or a small ladder stitch. Repeat on the opposite side of the quilt.

10 Cut a further two strips from the contrast fabric: 3 x 140cm (1¼ x 55in). Add the first of the remaining strips in the same way but remember to allow 1cm (½in) of excess binding to overlap at each end of the top of the quilt before stitching the strip to the front of the quilt.

11 Fold over the excess fabric at the end of the strip to make neat square corners and continue to finish as for the previous strip. Stitch the final strip to the bottom of the quilt in the same way.

12 Quilt each Template E group with full flower quilting motif Template F (given on the pull-out template at the back). Make a template from medium-weight iron-on interfacing. Fuse two pieces together, draw the motif onto the interfacing and carefully cut it out. Pin the design to the

quilting area and quilt around its edge. As it is flexible it is easy to stitch around and will last for a long time. If you want, you can tack (baste) it in place. Alternatively, you may want to quilt freehand.

13 For the calico (muslin) border, use the three-quarter flower motif (Template G) to quilt at each corner, and half-flower Template H to quilt a half flower at the half-way point on each edge, as shown on the plan below. I have used a variegated thread in pale green.

14 Refer to the plan below for quilting the rest of the border: I have used a half-circle to represent each additional half-flower border motif, which is made using Template I. Make several Template I half-flower motifs and set them out, working from the corners to the centre of the quilt along the inner edge first. Position the half-flowers evenly according to the space you have. Then set out the outer edge half motifs and quilt.

15 Stitch six button embellishments to each raised block or quilt the circle shapes if preferred.

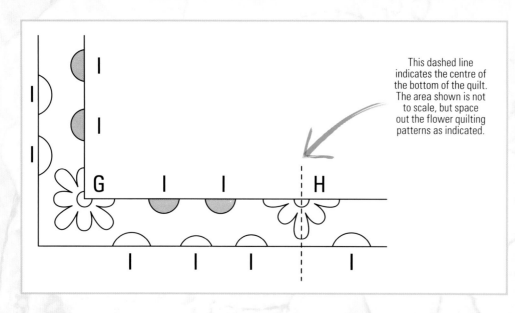

This dashed line indicates the centre of the bottom of the quilt. The area shown is not to scale, but space out the flower quilting patterns as indicated.

Quilt the Template G corner flowers and the central Template H half flowers first. Next quilt the Template I half flowers indicated by grey semi-circles, shown on the inner edge of the border, before finishing with further Template I half flowers, indicated by white semi-circles on the outer edge of the border.

The completed border with a mitred corner and quilted motifs.

▶ Variations

Pillow, measuring 41cm (16in) square.

The dahlia pattern stitched in self colour with added squares and circles shows an alternative way of designing the block. This pillow has a decorative stipple-quilted background.

Pillow, measuring 46cm (18in) square.

The dahlia patchwork templates have been enlarged and a border added to the centre square. A half dahlia design is used for quilting the blue triangles.

Silk dupion wedding ring pillow, measuring 23cm (9in) square.

This piece is stitched with turquoise and burnt orange variegated polyester thread and quilted with copper-coloured metallic thread.

Celtic Lotus wall hanging

▶ 58.5 x 79cm (23 x 31in)

This design started life as a doodle! Having scribbled the simple lines in biro, I set about developing the design on an A4 (21 x 29.7cm / 8¼ x 11¾in) sheet of 5mm (¼in) squared paper. Over the next two evenings the design materialised. The diamond shapes in the border evolved from an Egyptian mummified cat that I had seen in a museum. I had the design enlarged at a photocopy shop that specialises in printing architectural drawings; I have found this to be a very quick and useful way to see a scale drawing printed at full size. The pattern includes areas that can be machine stitched or stitched by hand.

You will need

- 75cm (29½in) of quilters' calico (muslin)
- 75cm (29½in) of butter muslin (cheesecloth)
- One piece of 92 x 71cm (36 x 28in) 2oz (57g) polyester wadding (batting)
- Two skeins of quilting wool
- Small bag of toy filler (or scraps of teased-out polyester wadding/batting)
- Sewing thread to match the colour of the wall hanging for sewing the design and quilting
- Tacking (basting) thread in pale blue, green or pink
- 5mm (¼in) wide low-tack, masking tape
- Sewing machine: it is advisable to stitch a small test piece first to see whether your machine works well with the fine fabrics – use a suitable needle – size 75 or 80
- 5mm (¼in) machine foot
- Needles
- Stuffing tool
- HB pencil

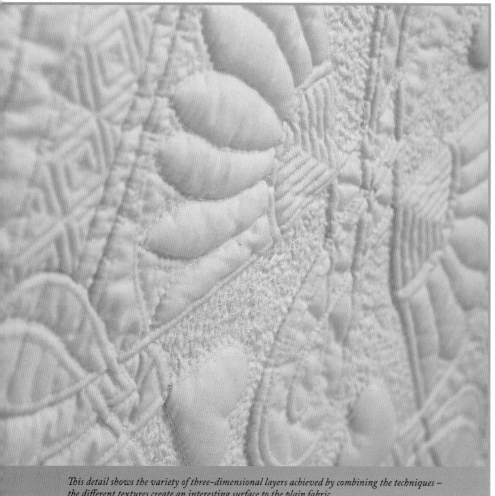

This detail shows the variety of three-dimensional layers achieved by combining the techniques – the different textures create an interesting surface to the plain fabric.

Three-dimensional quilting

1 The template shows just over one quarter of the whole design (the orange lines indicate the half-way points on each edge). You will need to carefully and selectively mirror image the shape to create the entire design, keeping the centre as it is, as it is not symmetrical, and then rotate it to fill in the missing parts. Cut the calico (muslin) into two 92 x 71cm (36 x 28in) rectangles. Put one piece aside. Secure the design to a flat surface and place a calico (muslin) piece directly on top of the design leaving an equal amount of fabric all the way around the pattern. Secure the fabric to the flat surface and lightly trace the solid lines of the design onto the fabric using the pencil. Remove the paper template after completing all of the design. Cut a 92 x 71cm (36 x 28in) rectangle from the butter muslin (cheesecloth). Pin, then tack (baste) the butter muslin (cheesecloth) to the back of the fabric with a 2.5cm (1in) grid and add a final row of tacking (basting) to the outer edge of the design, 1cm (½in) away from the edges of the pattern.

Template 2

Make this your initial
tape placement.

Make this your initial
tape placement.

Make this your initial
tape placement.

2 If you have chosen to machine stitch the basic lines, proceed as follows. Set the machine to a medium stitch length (about eleven stitches to 2.5cm/1in is ideal). Use a transparent foot on the machine so you can see to follow the design accurately. When stitching the lines, do not use the reverse to lock the stitches. Instead, leave enough thread at the start and end of each stitched line to take the upper thread through to the back of the work and tie it off with two knots. You should then cut the threads leaving tails of approximately 1cm (½in) – there is no need to sew the ends to neaten.

3 Stitch all the basic lines that have been drawn onto the fabric – you must stop and restart at each end of a line where the line appears to go over and under in the design. Start at the centre of the work and stitch slowly across the bias of the fabric and carefully manipulate the design around the curved shapes. Do not allow the fabric to gather when sewing the very small curves – keep it as flat as possible. Work your way to the outer edges. Neaten all the loose threads as you go along. Add an extra 5mm (¼in) line around the outside of the last rectangle.

4 If you are hand-stitching, start at the centre of the design and sew with backstitch all the basic lines, except the heart and the flower petal outlines, which will be sewn with running stitch. Use the 5mm (¼in) masking tape to make the parallel channels in the petal shapes and the flower centres and sew with backstitch. Stitch all the rectangle shapes in the same way to the outside edge of the work.

5 Use the masking tape as a guide for adding the extra lines in the diamond shapes for the border. Stitch with running stitch but backstitch all the tiny squares in the centre of the shapes. Sew all the extra lines with running stitch. Remove all the tacking (basting) from the work, leaving only those stitches that are on the outside edge of the pattern. Press both sides of the work.

6 Turn the work to the back and stuff only the pink areas shown on Template 3. Be careful not to over-stuff each of the larger shapes – you might need to make more than one hole in the butter muslin (cheesecloth) to enable you to access these areas.

7 Next you will complete the cording – refer back to Template 2. Remember, only cut a maximum length of 50cm (20in) of wool from the skein when you are threading the channels. Also if you have to join the wool only do so at the corners of a shape or at any 'V' shape that might appear within a design. Start in the centre of the design with the Italian quilting channels that you stitched first of all. Remember to follow the 'overs and unders' on the design – you can continue around the shape without having to cut the wool at each stopping and starting point for this design as it will not be too bulky or cause you problems when adding the final quilting.

8 Thread the curved shape on the flowerhead and petals that are inside the first rectangle border, followed by the straight lines in each petal, cutting the wool at either end of each channel. Thread the curve below the stuffed petals on the other two flowers. Next thread the chevron shapes. Leave a loop where the chevron changes direction and leave a tail at the end of each channel.

9 Thread the straight lines of each rectangle working from the inner one to the outside edge of the work. Leave tails or loops on each corner of every rectangle as required. If you are careful, you can use longer lengths of wool to thread into each rectangle. When using pre-shrunk wool, you need only leave loops on the corners of each line, but if it is not pre-shrunk, remember to leave a loop every 10cm (4in) along each channel. Complete the diamond border by threading every concentric channel separately within each shape, remembering to leave very small loops on each corner where the diamond changes direction. Thread the half diamonds either side of the centre shape leaving loops and tails. Always thread the inner channel first on multi-threaded designs.

10 Pin and tack (baste) the wadding (batting) and second piece of calico (muslin) to the back of the wall hanging in a grid formation. If you prefer, you could use a pale-coloured printed cotton fabric instead of the calico (muslin) for the backing fabric at this stage.

11 Refer to Template 3 for the quilting instructions. You need only quilt selected areas. Use the same thread that you used to stitch the design. Start in the middle of the work and echo quilt (outline the design) with the basic quilting stitch, 2mm (1/16in) away from the lines. Outline the heart shapes and the flower shapes in the central area of the pattern. Stitch in the ditch for the rest of the quilting, except the outside of the double channel border, which should have a row of echo quilting sewn along its outer edge. Add a further line of quilting all around the outer edge, through all the layers, 1cm (½in) away from the previous quilting. Use two rows of 5mm (¼in) masking tape side by side for this.

12 Stipple quilt the background that surrounds the central shape – use a large single stipple stitch in the areas indicated with pink dots. Start close to the centre and work to the outer edges. The size of the stitches for this background are approximately 5mm (¼in) long. You could quilt this area with meander quilting if you prefer (see page 27).

13 With a backstitch, quilt a 'Y' shape in the space above each stuffed petal on the two centre flower shapes.

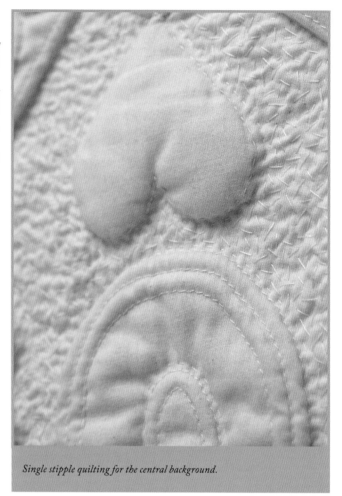

Single stipple quilting for the central background.

The corner flower and diamond border filled with parallel lines of French-style cording. See also the Egyptian inspiration section, page 123.

Making up

1 Work from the back of the hanging. Start with the two long sides and trim away a tiny amount of the backing fabric, wadding (batting) and butter muslin (cheesecloth) only, just outside the last quilting line, leaving just the calico (muslin) intact. Do this on all four sides of the work. Again, start with the long sides and fold the calico (muslin) over to the back of the work along the quilted edge. Turn under the raw edge and pin, then tack (baste) in place. With a small ladder stitch, sew this to the backing fabric to neaten. Repeat this along the top and bottom edges, then tuck each end in to neaten and to make square corners.

2 Make a hanging sleeve from the remaining calico (muslin) or your printed backing fabric. Cut a piece of fabric 60 x 14cm (23¾ x 5in). Fold under the short ends to the wrong side of the fabric by 1cm (½in). Press, then repeat. Stitch in place. Turn the long edges 1cm (½in) to the wrong side and press. With the right side of the fabric facing you, place it onto the back of the hanging with the long edge pinned 1cm (½in) down from the top edge of the hanging. The short ends should be equal distance inside the width of the hanging. Ladder stitch or hem stitch it to the back of the work along the long edge – do not let any stitches come through and show on the right side of the work. Pin the other long sleeve edge flat against the back of the work and sew the lower edge to the back of the hanging as before. You will now have a 'tube' on the back of the work so that you can hang it on the wall with a pole or batten. You could make a sleeve for the lower edge of the hanging if you want to add weight to the work. This wall hanging can hang either vertically or horizontally – the choice is yours.

Here you can see the 'overs and unders' in the centre of the design, the chevron parallel rows in the flowers and the backstitched 'Y' shapes above the petals.

75

Acanthus Entwined table runner

84 x 38cm (33 x 15in)

While looking through my 'sketchbook stash' for inspiration, I found a very old pencil drawing traced onto greaseproof paper that had been taken from a photograph of a doormat with interlaced circles. It reminded me of wrought ironwork and celtic designs. I used the acanthus plant that grows in my garden for inspiration for the circles, and for the designs either side of the centre. I enlarged and refined the sketch to see if this was a possibility and decided to incorporate the curved pattern into either end of the piece to make it more interesting.

You will need

- 50cm (20in) of quilters' calico (muslin) for the front and back of the table runner
- 50cm (20in) of butter muslin (cheesecloth)
- Two 94 x 50cm (37 x 20in) pieces of 2oz (57g) Thermore wadding (batting) – this is flatter but still retains the bounce or 'loft' required to make the techniques successful
- Two skeins of quilting wool
- Small bag of toy filler (or scraps of teased-out polyester wadding/batting)
- Sewing thread for sewing the design and quilting
- Tacking (basting) thread in pale blue, green or pink
- 5mm (¼in) reel of low-tack, masking tape
- Needles
- Stuffing tool
- HB pencil

Three-dimensional quilting

Template 1, see also full-size pull-out template

Make this your initial
tape placement.

1 Cut the calico (muslin) into two 94 x 50cm (37 x 20in) rectangles. Put one piece aside. Secure the design to a flat surface and place the calico (muslin) directly on top of the design, leaving an equal amount of fabric all the way around the pattern. Secure the fabric to the flat surface and lightly trace the design onto the fabric using the pencil, including the dots shown in red at either end of the long sides, see Template 1, page 76. Remove the paper template. Cut the butter muslin (cheesecloth) into two 94 x 50cm (37 x 20in) rectangles and put one piece aside. Tack (baste) one piece of butter muslin (cheesecloth) to the back of the fabric with a 2.5cm (1in) grid and add a final row of tacking (basting) to the outer edge of the design 1cm (½in) away from the perimeter edges of the pattern. Stitch all the basic lines that have been drawn onto the fabric with running stitch.

2 Use Template 2 and add the extra lines of stitching where indicated. This illustration shows a portion of the design – repeat the techniques throughout. Use the masking tape to create the 5mm (¼in) channels. You can carefully bend the tape around the curved shapes where necessary. Sew all the extra lines with running stitch. Remove all the tacking (basting) stitches from the work except the stitches on the outside edge of the pattern. Press both sides of the work.

3 Turn the work to the back and stuff only the areas shown in pink on Template 3. Be careful not to over-stuff each of the larger shapes – you might need to make more than one hole in the butter muslin (cheesecloth) for access.

4 Next you will create the cording – return to Template 2. Remember, only cut a maximum length of 46cm (18in) of wool from the skein when you are threading the channel, unless told otherwise. Also if you have to join the wool, only do so at the corners of a shape or at any 'V' shape that might appear within a design. Start with the channels surrounding the stuffed shapes in the central motif. Then thread the straight lines in the centre of the design leaving a tail at either end. Continue and complete the two channels that surround the centre motif, remembering to leave very small loops where the design changes direction – the indentations where the half-circle shapes along the soft curves meet. Thread the inner channel first. Leave tails at either end for the double channels that form the entwined curves and appear to go over and under themselves. These also form the outside edge of the table runner. Finally, thread the small channels that are at the base of the stem of the acanthus leaf and the remaining chevron channels at the top of the leaf.

5 Pin and tack (baste) the two pieces of wadding (batting) – as a double layer – and butter muslin (cheesecloth) to the back of the runner with grid tacking (basting) as before.

6 Refer to Template 3 for the quilting; you need only quilt selected areas. Use the same thread that you used to stitch the design. Start in the middle of the flower shapes and stitch in the ditch with the basic quilting stitch: if you follow the direction shown you will be able to work in a continuous line, which will create four overlapping circles. Next, stitch in the ditch between the second and third channels that surround the centre, followed by quilting just outside the fourth row for the centre shape. Quilt inside the circles, around the acanthus leaves and either side of the double channel that forms the edge of the runner. It is advisable to quilt from the centre of the work and sew towards the outer edge where possible; therefore some of the quilting might have to stop and start – if this happens, I leave extra thread where I need to stop and then re-thread when I return to the area and continue quilting the shape.

7 Stipple quilt the background with a large double stipple stitch in the areas indicated with pink dots. Start close to the centre and work to the outside edges. The size of the stitches for this background are approximately 1cm (½in) long. You could quilt this area with a 2cm (¾in) cross-hatch pattern if you prefer.

8 Finally, use the masking tape as a guide and quilt through all the layers 5mm (¼in) away from the outside edge all around the runner. Remove the tacking (basting) threads from the work.

Here you can see the double stipple stitch used for the background – the larger stitch complements the scale of the motifs.

The table runner has shaped ends that reflect the shapes within the design, making it more interesting.

Making up

1 To keep the fabric layers in place while you trim, tack (baste) with a small stitch all around the runner, through all the layers, 1cm (½in) outside the last quilted line. Trim all the fabrics just outside this line. Remove the tacking (basting). Start with the two long sides and carefully cut into the calico (muslin) edge at the angle shown on the full-size pattern. Trim away the wadding (batting) and butter muslin (cheesecloth) a tiny distance outside the quilting line, between the red dots at either end of each side. Fold the calico (muslin) to the back of the work along the quilted edge. Pin in place and with a small running stitch, sew this into the wadding (batting) at the back of the runner close to the raw edge – tuck each cut end in to neaten. Re-quilt along the outside edge of the channel through all the layers. Repeat on the other long side.

2 For the shaped ends, cut away the wadding (batting) and butter muslin (cheesecloth) as before. Start with the large semi-circular shape and carefully fold the calico (muslin) over to the back of the work along the quilting line that edges the outer channel – this will be a bit fiddly at first as there will be a little wadding (batting) and butter muslin (cheesecloth) remaining under the calico (muslin) – pin as you go, working from the middle of the semi-circle towards the dip that joins it to the next one.

3 Very carefully make a straight cut through the calico (muslin) towards the dip, as close as possible without cutting into the stitching on the front of the design – about 4mm (³/₁₆in) from the quilting just outside the channel. This will allow the calico (muslin) to fold over neatly at each of the 'dips' following the outer shape to give a good finish. Tack (baste) in place. Continue working in this way for the next two semi-circular shapes. Stitch the calico (muslin) to the wadding (batting) to neaten as before, but stitch just below the quilted line where you trimmed away the excess wadding (batting). You might have to make small gathers along the convex curves. Repeat this on the other half of the shaped end. Neaten the other end in the same way.

4 Pin the backing fabric to the back of the runner and cut it 5mm (¼in) larger than the front, all the way round. If you prefer, you can back the runner with a pale-coloured cotton printed fabric. Unpin the backing fabric, then turn the excess backing fabric under by 1cm (½in) on the long sides. Repin it and tack (baste) in place. Turn under the backing fabric on the shaped ends enough to cover the pre-neatened calico (muslin) and to ensure that the 'dips' are covered too. Pin, tack (baste) and with a small ladder stitch sew the backing in place. To complete the work, remove the tacking (basting) and catch the backing to the runner with a small stitch through the centre of each of the large, circular motifs.

The centre motif showing the selective quilting that creates the overlapping circles.

The background texture contrasts with the stylised trapunto acanthus leaf shape, and gives a low relief sculptured feel to the work.

The inner double channels of Italian quilting are stitched in the ditch to separate them from the outer channels – doubling the channels gives strength to the design and balances the strong shapes within the areas.

Ivory Splendour sampler quilt

► 137 x 137cm (54 x 54in)

Quilts that are composed of blocks made from a variety of designs and techniques are known as 'sampler quilts'. The blocks are usually separated from each other by a strip of fabric, or sashing, that acts as a border to each design. I have designed nine different blocks that explore the raised corded and stuffed work. Four of the blocks are variations based on an eight-pointed star, two contain simple squares, one contains a circle that I divided into six segments and the two interlaced circle designs were inspired from an embossed design on a paper kitchen roll!

If you do not want to make a quilt, each block could become a pillow front or other item instead, or you might like to select just a few of the designs and make a quilt from these. I suggest that you allow a 46cm (18in) square of fabric per block. The patterns are 42.5cm (16¾in) square and by the time the final quilting is completed they become around 39.5cm (15½in). Each block is made and quilted individually and they are joined with sashing into three strips, then backed with a pale-coloured printed fabric. Each strip is joined together using the quilt-as-you-go method with the sashing quilted after each strip is joined together. The intersections have been embellished with fancy pearl buttons – this is optional – I have added them because some of the blocks have been embellished with beads.

As you might like to make the sashing wider, or add an extra border to the quilt, the yardage is given in two parts. If you decide to stitch the main design with a coloured thread you could use coloured sashing to match, which would give the quilt a totally different appearance. Do not forget, however, that the final quilting must be carried out in the background colour for the blocks unless you choose to use a metallic thread.

You will need

For the nine blocks you will need:

- 2.5m (2¾ yds) quilters' calico (muslin), 112cm (44in) wide
- 5m (5½ yds) of butter muslin (cheesecloth), 1m (39in) wide
- 1m (39in) of 2oz (57g) polyester wadding (batting), 283cm (102in) wide: Polydown cut from the bolt is the best to use
- Nine skeins of quilting wool: pre-shrunk is best
- Bag of toy filler (or scraps of teased-out polyester wadding/batting)
- Sewing thread to match the colour of the calico (muslin) for stitching and quilting
- Tacking (basting) thread in pale blue, green or pink
- 5mm (¼in) wide low-tack, masking tape
- 1cm (½in) wide low-tack masking tape
- 2m (2¼ yds) backing fabric, 150cm (60in) wide
- Sewing machine for making up the quilt with a 5mm (¼in) foot and a zipper foot
- Needles
- Stuffing tool
- HB pencil

Any additional items needed will be given at the beginning of each block

For the sashing that includes the outer border you will need:

- 1.5m (1¾ yds) quilters' calico (muslin)
- 3m (3½ yds) butter muslin (cheesecloth)
- 50cm (20in) polyester wadding (batting)
- Sixteen 2cm (¾in) flat 2- or 4-hole buttons (optional). Do not use shank buttons as these will stand away from the quilt when sewn in place

Three-dimensional quilting

► FOR EACH BLOCK:

1 Where designs are symmetrical they are given as quarters and halves: these will need mirror imaging to create the entire design. Instruction is given with each block.

2 Cut one 46 x 46cm (18 x 18in) square of quilters' calico (muslin). Cut two 46 x 46cm (18 x 18in) squares of butter muslin (cheesecloth). Cut one 46 x 46cm (18 x 18in) square of wadding (batting). Secure Template 1 to a flat surface and place the calico (muslin) directly on top of the design, leaving an equal amount of fabric all the way around the pattern. Secure the fabric to the surface and lightly trace the design onto the fabric with the pencil. Remove the paper template.

3 Pin, then tack (baste) one piece of butter muslin (cheesecloth) to the back of the fabric with a 2.5cm (1in) grid and add a final row of tacking (basting) to the outer edge of the design, 1cm (½in) away from the perimeter edges of the pattern.

Top row, left to right, Blocks 1–3.

Middle row, left to right, Blocks 4–6.

Bottom row, left to right, Blocks 7–9.

84

▶ BLOCK 1: FESTOON STAR

Additional items required: a small pack of transparent glass seed beads, beading needle and beading thread

1 The template given is for a quarter of the design; you will need to mirror it to create the full design. Stitch all of the main design with running stitch.

2 Look at Template 2 and add the extra lines of stitching where indicated. Use the masking tape to create the 5mm (¼in) channels. Finish by creating two channels on the outer edge of the block. Sew all the extra lines with running stitch. Remove all the tacking (basting) stitches from the work, leaving only those stitches that are on the outside edge of the pattern. Press both sides of the work.

3 Turn the work to the back and stuff only the pink areas shown on Template 3. Be careful not to over-stuff each of the shapes.

4 To cord the shape, return to Template 2. Start in the centre of the design and add small loops where the star shape changes direction. Thread each channel separately. Start and finish with a tail approximately 5mm (¼in) long.

5 Thread the parallel rows of the large star shape leaving loops as before; thread each row separately. Thread all the remaining channels and finally fill the two rows on the outside edge of the block. If you are careful, you can use longer lengths of wool to thread each outside row. When using pre-shrunk wool, you need only leave loops on the corners of each square.

6 Pin and tack (baste) the wadding (batting) and second piece of butter muslin (cheesecloth) to the back of the block with grid tacking (basting).

7 Use Template 3 for quilting. You need only quilt selected areas. Use the same thread that you used to stitch the design. Start in the middle of the work and sew with the basic quilting stitch just outside the main stitched design elements. Stitch in the ditch where necessary.

8 To finish, stitch a row of seed beads close to the centre shape along the quilted line (see page 95 for reference). Stitch individual beads through all the layers to the background area where indicated with blue dots on Template 3. Write the block number on a small piece of paper and pin it to the block with a safety pin. Put the work to one side.

Top right-hand corner

Template 1, see also full-size pull-out template

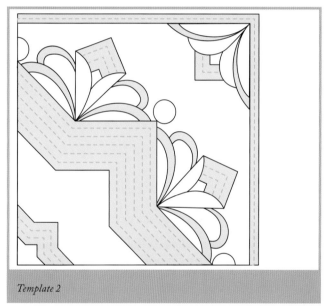

Template 2

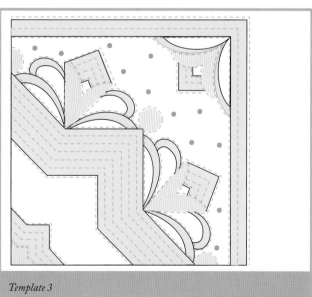

Template 3

Stuffing tip

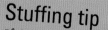

If the narrow parts of the shapes are difficult to stuff, go to the front of the work and push a sharp long needle into the stuffing close to the narrow section, hold it perpendicular to the fabric and pivot the needle towards the narrow part – this drags the stuffing into the empty space. Do this a couple of times and the space will fill.

► BLOCK 2: STAR SHINE

1 The template given is for a quarter of the design; you will need to mirror it to create the full design. Stitch the main design with running stitch and backstitch all of the small motifs within each triangle shape, also the shapes that are formed between the large petals in the centre on Template 1.

2 Using Template 2, add the extra lines of stitching as shown. Use the masking tape to create the 5mm (¼in) channels. Finish by creating the two channels on the outer edge of the block. Sew all the extra lines with running stitch. Remove all the tacking (basting) from the work, leaving only those stitches that are on the outside edge of the pattern. Press both sides of the work.

3 Turn the work to the back and stuff only the pink areas shown on Template 3. Be careful not to over-stuff the shapes. If the narrow parts on the shapes are difficult to stuff, follow the stuffing tip given on page 85.

4 To cord the design, return to Template 2. Start in the centre and add small loops when changing direction throughout the work. Thread the eight-pointed star – starting with the inside channel first. Thread the inside channel of the next eight points, following the triangle shapes between the star points. Then go back to fill each of the parallel channels that are inside the eight points. Start and finish with a tail approximately 5mm (¼in) long. Thread the channels within every other triangle shape and the four diagonal lines on each corner. Finally, fill the two rows on the outside edge of the block, as on Block 1 (see page 85).

5 Pin and tack (baste) the wadding (batting) and second piece of butter muslin (cheesecloth) to the back of the block with grid tacking (basting).

6 Use Template 3 for quilting. You need only quilt selected areas. Use the same thread that you used to stitch the design. Start in the middle of the work and sew with the basic quilting stitch just outside the main stitched design and stitch in the ditch where necessary. Finish with single stipple quilting at each corner, as shown on the template with pink dots. Make each stitch about 1cm (½in) long.

7 Write the block number on a small piece of paper and pin it to the block with a safety pin. Put the work to one side.

Top right-hand corner

Template 1, see also full-size pull-out template

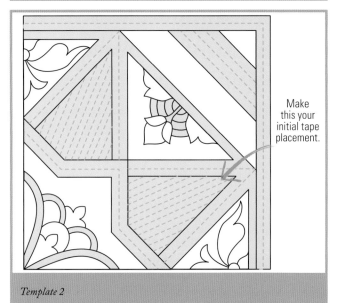

Make this your initial tape placement.

Template 2

Template 3

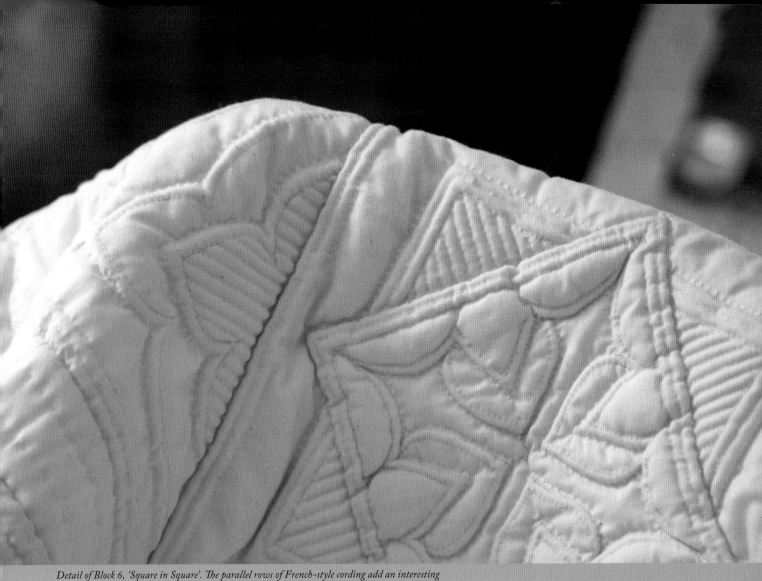

Detail of Block 6, 'Square in Square'. The parallel rows of French-style cording add an interesting texture to the block and by quilting only on the outside of each of the subsequent shapes, the block gives the illusion of several layers of fabric.

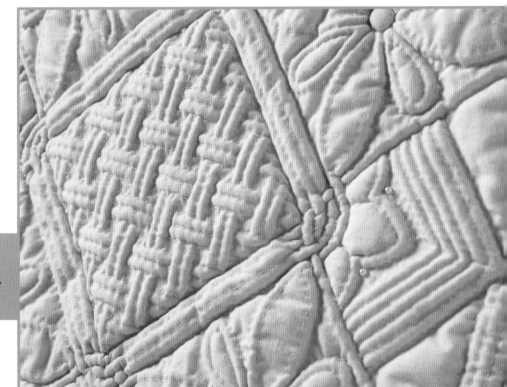

Detail of Block 4, 'Celtic Basket'. The corners of the basket interlace with the next square pattern to bring the design together. Quilting only along the outside of the large petals gives the impression of the centres being stuffed – in fact these are left empty and create another layer to the work.

Template 1, see also full-size pull-out template

Top

► BLOCK 3: INTERLACED CIRCLES

1 Because the design cannot be exactly quartered, Template 1 is given as a half, and must be mirrored to give the whole design. Stitch the main design with running stitch and carefully follow the overs and unders.

2 Use Template 2 and add the additional lines of stitching as shown. Use the masking tape to create the 5mm (¼in) channels. The tape will easily bend around the curved shapes. Finish with three channels on the outer edge of the block. Sew all the extra lines with running stitch. Remove all the tacking (basting) stitches from the work, leaving only those that are on the outside edge of the pattern. Press both sides of the work.

3 Turn the work to the back and stuff only the pink areas shown on Template 3. Be careful not to over-stuff the shapes. If the narrow parts on the shapes are difficult to stuff, follow the stuffing tip given on page 85.

4 To cord, start in the centre of the design and thread each circle separately. Thread the two curved channels that sit outside the eight large overlapping circles. Add small loops when changing direction on these rows. Next thread the parallel channels inside the eight petal shapes formed by the circles. Start and finish each one with a tail approximately 5mm (¼in) long. Thread the heart shape and parallel rows at each corner of the design. Finally fill the remaining three rows on the outside edge.

5 Pin and tack (baste) the wadding (batting) and second piece of butter muslin (cheesecloth) to the back of the block with grid tacking (basting).

6 Use Template 3 for quilting. Use the same thread that you used to stitch the design. Start in the middle of the work and sew with the basic quilting stitch and stitch in the ditch where necessary. You might want to fill the background with optional cross-hatch quilting, as shown.

7 Write the block number on a small piece of paper and pin it to the block with a safety pin. Put the work to one side.

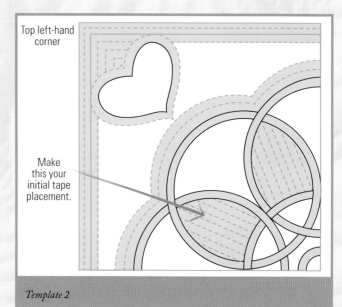

Top left-hand corner

Make this your initial tape placement.

Template 2

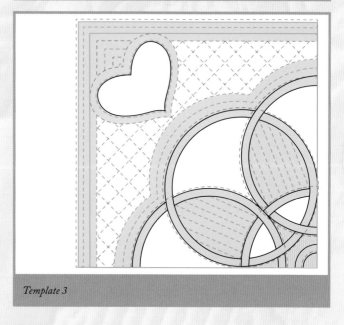

Template 3

Template 1, see also full-size pull-out template

Bottom right-
hand corner

Template 2

Template 3

▶ BLOCK 4: CELTIC BASKET

Additional items required: eight 3mm (¹/₈in) pearl beads, beading needle and thread

1 The template given is for a quarter of the design; you will need to mirror it to create the full design. However, please note that the square basket centre cannot be mirrored and so is given as a complete square on the pull-out template – it must be used as such for the overs and unders to work. Stitch the main design with running stitch and use backstitch on all the interlaced overs and unders on the corners of the basket and the looped shapes that appear to attach the squares to the framework, ensuring that all the overs and unders are followed correctly.

2 Use Template 2 and add the additional lines of stitching as shown. Use the masking tape to create the 5mm (¼in) channels. Finish with three channels on the outer edge of the block. Sew all the extra lines with running stitch. Remove all the tacking (basting) stitches from the work, leaving only those stitches that are on the outside edge of the pattern. Press both sides of the work.

3 Turn the work to the back and stuff only the pink areas shown on Template 3. Be careful not to over-stuff each of the shapes.

4 To cord, return to Template 2. Start in the centre of the design with the lines that surround the basket and make sure the unders and overs are followed at each corner. Thread each channel separately that forms the square basket pattern in the centre of the block. Next thread the flowers at each corner and add small loops to the ends of the pointed petals only. Next thread the square shapes that surround the flowers and all the remaining channels, finishing with the three rows on the outside edge.

5 Pin and tack (baste) the wadding (batting) and second piece of butter muslin (cheesecloth) to the back of the block with grid tacking (basting).

6 Use Template 3 for quilting. Use the same thread that you used to stitch the design. Start in the middle of the work and continue to the outside edge with the basic quilting stitch and stitch in the ditch where necessary. I have backstitched the interlaced corners and loops to emphasise the design (see page 87).

7 Finish by adding the eight pearl beads where shown – these are indicated with blue dots on Template 3. Stitch them securely though all the fabric layers.

8 Write the block number on a small piece of paper and pin it to the block with a safety pin. Put the work to one side.

Template 1, see also full-size pull-out template

Top left-hand corner

Make this your initial tape placement.

Template 2

Template 3

▶ BLOCK 5: HEARTS AND RINGS

1 This design is not precisely symmetrical, due to the positioning of the under and overs, so is given as a whole. Stitch the main design lines with running stitch.

2 Use Template 2 and add the additional lines of stitching as shown. Use the masking tape to create the 5mm (¼in) channels. The tape will easily bend around the curved shapes. Sew all the extra lines with running stitch. Remove all the tacking (basting) stitches from the work, leaving only those that are on the outside edge of the pattern. Press both sides of the work.

3 Turn the work to the back and stuff only the pink areas shown on Template 3. Be careful not to over-stuff the shapes.

4 To cord, return to Template 2. Start in the middle of the design and thread the small circle, then the large circle. Thread the six large interlaced circles next, following the overs and unders as you go. Then thread each concentric circle. Thread the outside of the heart shape – start at the indent and work around the shape, remembering to leave a loop at the point. Next go back to fill each of the parallel channels separately that are inside the heart shape. Start and finish with a tail approximately 5mm (¼in) long. Finally fill the two rows on the outside edge of the block.

5 Pin and tack (baste) the wadding (batting) and second piece of butter muslin (cheesecloth) to the back of the block with grid tacking (basting).

6 Use Template 3 for quilting. Use the same thread that you used to stitch the design. Start in the middle of the work and sew with the basic quilting stitch and stitch in the ditch where necessary. Backstitch to quilt where the channels meet to emphasise the overs and unders. Echo quilt around the outside of the circles and hearts 2mm (¹/₈in) away from the corded line.

7 Write the block number on a small piece of paper and pin it to the block with a safety pin. Put the work to one side.

90

► BLOCK 6: SQUARE IN SQUARE

1 The template given is for a quarter of the design; you will need to mirror it to create the full design. Stitch the main design with running stitch.

2 Use Template 2 and add the additional lines of stitching as shown. Use the masking tape to create the 5mm (¼in) channels. Finish with two channels on the outer edge of the block. Sew all the extra lines with running stitch. Remove all the tacking (basting) stitches from the work, leaving only those stitches that are on the outside edge of the pattern. Press both sides of the work.

3 Turn the work to the back and stuff only the pink areas shown on Template 2. Be careful not to over-stuff the shapes.

4 To cord, start in the centre of the design and add small loops when changing direction throughout the work. The wool will easily thread into the very narrow channels, if you ease it through carefully. When threading double channels, fill the inside row first. Continue to the outside edge of the design, then go back to fill each of the multiple lines separately within the parallel channel areas. Start and finish with a tail approximately 5mm (¼in) long. Finally fill the two rows on the outside edge of the block.

5 Pin and tack (baste) the wadding (batting) and second piece of butter muslin (cheesecloth) to the back of the block with grid tacking (basting).

6 Use Template 3 for quilting. Use the same thread that you used to stitch the design. Start in the middle of the work and sew with the basic quilting stitch and stitch in the ditch where necessary. Echo quilt the motifs on the corners of the design 2mm (¹/₈in) away from the corded edge.

7 Write the block number on a small piece of paper and pin it to the block with a safety pin. Put the work to one side.

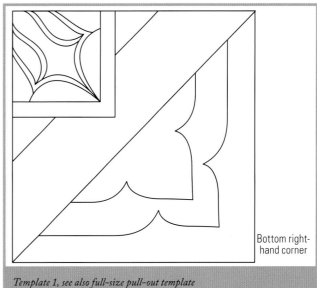

Bottom right-hand corner

Template 1, see also full-size pull-out template

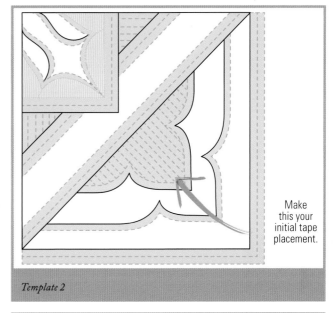

Make this your initial tape placement.

Template 2

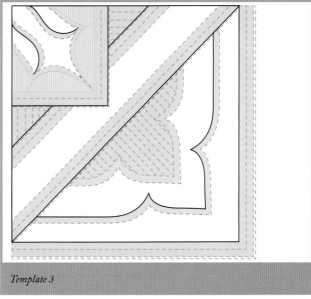

Template 3

91

▶ BLOCK 7: MUSK ROSE

1 The template given is for a quarter of the design; you will need to mirror it to create the full design. Stitch the main design with running stitch.

2 Use Template 2 and add the additional lines of stitching as shown. Use the masking tape to create the 5mm (¼in) channels. Finish with three channels on the outer edge of the block. Sew all the extra lines with running stitch. Remove all the tacking (basting) from the work, leaving only those stitches that are on the outside edge of the pattern. Press both sides.

3 Turn the work to the back and stuff only the pink areas shown on Template 3. Be careful not to over-stuff the shapes. If the narrow parts on the shapes are difficult to stuff, follow the stuffing tip given on page 85.

4 To cord, return to Template 2. Start in the centre of the design and thread the petals. Next thread the outside channel on each of the large petal shapes, then go back to fill each of the parallel channels separately that are inside the six petals. Start and finish with a tail approximately 5mm (¼in) long. Thread the two heart shapes that are between the large petals and leave a small loop at the indentations. Thread the large circle, then the corner motifs, leaving loops where necessary. Finally fill the three rows on the outside edge of the block.

5 Pin and tack (baste) the wadding (batting) and second piece of butter muslin (cheesecloth) to the back of the block with grid tacking (basting).

6 Use Template 3 for quilting. Use the same thread that you used to stitch the design. Start in the middle of the work and sew a backstitch to emphasise the centre of the flower. Stitch in the ditch around the outside of this flower shape and outside the large petals. Echo quilt around the two heart shapes and outside the large circle, and the corner motif, 2mm (¹⁄₈in) away from the corded edge. Stitch in the ditch along the corner shapes where indicated. Then inside and outside of the three channels on the outside of the design.

7 Write the block number on a small piece of paper and pin it to the block with a safety pin. Put the work to one side.

Bottom right-hand corner

Template 1, see also full-size pull-out template

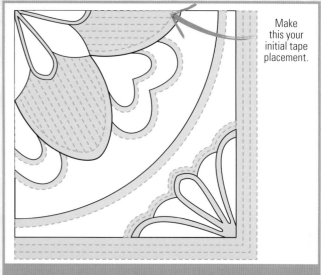

Make this your initial tape placement.

Template 2

Template 3

92

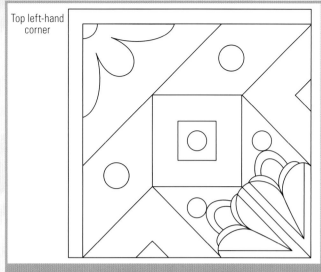

Top left-hand corner

Template 1, see also full-size pull-out template

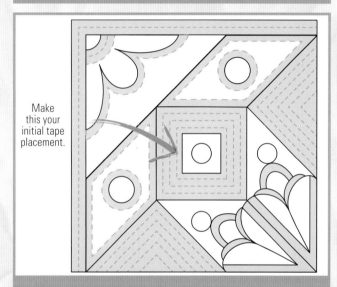

Make this your initial tape placement.

Template 2

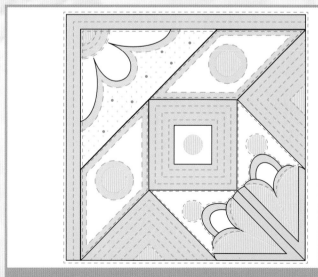

Template 3

▶ BLOCK 8: SQUARE DANCE

1 The template given is for a quarter of the design; you will need to mirror it to create the full design. Stitch the main design with running stitch.

2 Use Template 2 and add the additional lines of stitching as shown. Use the masking tape to create the 5mm (¼in) channels. Finish with two channels on the outer edge of the block. Sew all the extra lines with running stitch. Remove all the tacking (basting) stitches from the work, leaving only those stitches that are on the outside edge of the pattern. Press both sides of the work.

3 Turn the work to the back and stuff only the pink areas shown on Template 3. Be careful not to over-stuff the shapes. If the narrow parts on the shapes are difficult to stuff, follow the stuffing tip given on page 85. If the tapered shape is very narrow at its end, you can thread a short length of wool into this part and bury the ends in the stuffing.

4 To cord, return to Template 2. Start in the centre of the design and thread the two channels on each petal shape, adding small loops when changing direction throughout the work. Thread the eight small shapes that appear between the petals – starting with the inside channel first. Thread the concentric squares beginning with the smallest one and gradually work to the largest one – thread each square separately. Next thread the channel around the stuffed circle, then the diamond shape, and continue with the corners. Finally fill the two rows on the outside edge of the block.

5 Pin and tack (baste) the wadding (batting) and second piece of butter muslin (cheesecloth) to the back of the block with grid tacking (basting).

6 Use Template 3 for quilting. Use the same thread that you used to stitch the design. Start in the middle of the work and sew a couple of small backstitches through the centre of the flower shape to pull the centre down. Continue quilting the areas indicated on the guide with the basic quilting stitch, just outside of the main stitched design and stitch in the ditch where necessary. Quilt to the outer edge of the block. Finish with small single stipple quilting at each corner, as indicated with pink dots. Make each stipple stitch about 3mm (⅛in) long. The blue dots marked indicate where I added beads. Create a backstitch star shape in the very centre of the block to complete.

7 Write the block number on a small piece of paper and pin it to the block with a safety pin. Put the work to one side.

93

Top right-hand corner

Template 1, see also full-size pull-out template

Template 2

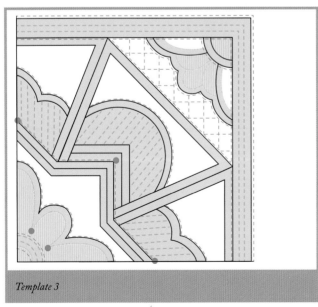

Template 3

▶ BLOCK 9: STAR FLOWER

Additional items required: sixteen 5mm (¼in) pearl beads, beading needle and thread

1 The template given is for a quarter of the design; you will need to mirror it to create the full design. Stitch the main design with running stitch.

2 Use Template 2 and add the additional lines of stitching as shown. Use the masking tape to create the 5mm (¼in) channels. Finish with three channels on the outer edge of the block. Sew all the extra lines with running stitch. Remove all the tacking (basting) stitches from the work, leaving only those stitches that are on the outside edge of the pattern. Press both sides of the work.

3 Turn the work to the back and stuff only the pink areas shown on Template 3. Be careful not to over-stuff the shapes. The tapered shape at the corner is very narrow at its end – you can thread a short length of wool into this part and bury the ends in the stuffing.

4 To cord, return to Template 2. Start in the centre of the design and thread the two channels surrounding the stuffed centre. Continue working towards the outer edge of the design, not forgetting to add small loops when changing direction throughout the work. Thread the eight-pointed star – start with the inside channel. Thread the double channels of the next eight-pointed star, then the radiating lines that make the trapezium shapes. Thread the channels that form the rounded shapes inside of the trapeziums then thread the parallel channels separately. Start and finish with a tail approximately 5mm (¼in) long. Thread the four corners and finally fill the three rows on the outside edge of the block.

5 Pin and tack (baste) the wadding (batting) and second piece of butter muslin (cheesecloth) to the back of the block with grid tacking (basting).

6 Use Template 3 for quilting. Use the same thread that you used to stitch the design. Start in the middle of the work and sew with the basic quilting stitch just outside the main stitched design and stitch in the ditch where necessary. Quilt to the outside edge of the block. Finish with cross-hatch quilting at each corner, as shown. Use the 1cm (½in) tape; stitch the vertical lines first, then the horizontal lines.

7 Finally, sew the pearl beads in place through all the layers, as indicated with blue dots on Template 3. Write the block number on a small piece of paper and pin it to the block with a safety pin. Put the work to one side.

8 All nine blocks are now complete and you are now ready to add the sashing.

Preparing the blocks

Check that each finished block is the same size. Make sure there is a line of quilting on the outside edge of each block close to the last threaded channel on the pattern. With your sewing machine, fitted with its 5mm (¼in) foot and using a medium to large straight stitch, sew through all the layers 5mm (¼in) away from the final quilting. Repeat this again and stitch another 5mm (¼in) away from the previous row of machine stitching. This will stabilise the layers and you should now have 1cm (½in) from the final quilting to this last line of stitching all around the block. This is the seam allowance. Keeping the last row of machine stitching intact, trim away the excess fabric beyond this point, close to the last stitched line. Repeat this for all nine blocks. Each block should now measure 42.5cm (16¾in) square.

Detail of Block 1, 'Festoon Star', showing the small beads stitched into the centre along the quilted line.

Making up

It is a good idea to pin each block, in order, to a cotton sheet or a design wall if you have one. You can then see how the quilt will look when finished and it will prevent you accidentally sewing the wrong blocks together. The numbers should remain in place until the nine blocks are put together. The seam allowance is 1cm (½in) throughout.

For the sashing and border you will need to cut:

- Twenty-four strips from the quilters' calico (muslin): 42.5 x 7.5cm (16¾ x 3in)
- Sixteen squares from the quilters' calico (muslin): 7.5 x 7.5cm (3 x 3in)
- Thirty-six strips from the butter muslin (cheesecloth): 42.5 x 7.5cm (16¾ x 3in)
- Sixteen squares from the butter muslin (cheesecloth): 7.5 x 7.5cm (3 x 3in)
- Four strips of butter muslin (cheesecloth): 138 x 7.5cm (54½ x 3in)
- Twelve strips from the polyester wadding (batting): 42.5 x 7.5cm (16¾ x 3in)
- Four strips from the polyester wadding (batting): 138 x 7.5cm (54½ x 3in)

1 Take four 42.5 x 7.5cm (16¾ x 3in) calico (muslin) strips and four 42.5 x 7.5cm (16¾ x 3in) butter muslin (cheesecloth) strips. Add one butter muslin (cheesecloth) strip to the back of each calico (muslin) strip and tack (baste) together 1cm (½in) from the edge of the fabrics – all the way around.

2 With the zipper foot, or cording foot, on the machine, first pin and tack (baste), then sew with 1cm (½in) seam allowance one sashing strip created in step 1 to either side of Block 1 and Block 3 along the tacking (basting) lines, making sure that the stitching is close to the last quilted line along the edge of the channel for each block. Do not stitch into the channel! Join the sashing strips to either side of Block 2: this creates Row 1 of your quilt.

3 As in step 1, tack (baste) together four 7.5 x 7.5cm (3 x 3in) squares and three 42.5 x 7.5cm (16¾ x 3in) strips of butter muslin (cheesecloth) and calico (muslin). Sew together the squares and strips end to end with a 1cm (½in) seam allowance to form a long strip. Take care that the squares and strips line up perfectly with the lower edge of Row 1 – adjust if necessary. Pin and tack (baste) in place along the bottom of Row 1.

4 Pin and tack (baste) in place, then with the zipper, or cording foot on the machine, take a 1cm (½in) seam allowance and sew the long sashing strip created in step 3 to the bottom of Row 1. Sew along the tacking (basting) line, making sure that the stitching is as close to the last quilted line along the edges of the channels on each block as before.

5 Follow step 3 to make a sashing strip in the same way for the top of Row 1 and stitch in place, as shown below.

| Block 1 | Block 2 | Block 3 |

6 Follow steps 1 and 2 to sew together Blocks 4, 5 and 6 with sashing strips to create Row 2. Follow step 3 to make another sashing strip and stitch this to the bottom of Row 2 in the same way.

7 Follow steps 1 and 2 to sew together Blocks 7, 8 and 9 with sashing strips to create Row 3. Follow step 3 to make another sashing strip and stitch to the bottom of Row 3 in the same way.

8 Join Row 2 to the bottom of Row 1, checking that the blocks and the sashing line up.

9 Take one 138 x 7.5cm (54½ x 3in) strip of polyester wadding (batting) and trim to 5cm (2in) wide. Position on the back of the sashing between Rows 1 and 2. Tuck it under the long edges of the seam allowance and tack (baste) in place.

10 Take one 138 x 7.5cm (54½ x 3in) strip of butter muslin (cheesecloth) and place this on top of the wadding (batting) strip applied in step 9. Turn under the seam allowance on each long edge. Pin, then with running stitch, sew to the butter muslin (cheesecloth) on the back of the row in the same way.

11 Join Row 3 to the bottom of Row 2, and complete steps 9 and 10 to add another strip of wadding (batting) and butter muslin (cheesecloth) between Rows 2 and 3.

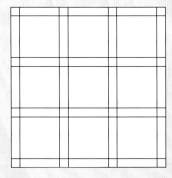

The nine joined blocks with corresponding sashing strips in place.

12 To finish the top of Row 1 continue as follows: trim a 138 x 7.5cm (54½ x 3in) strip of polyester wadding (batting) to 6.5cm (2½in) wide. Fit the strip to the back of the sashing at the top of Row 1. Tuck the wadding (batting) under the long edge of the seam allowance next to the blocks as before and tack (baste) in place. Lay the other edge on top of the sashing and tack (baste) all the layers together along the seam allowance line.

13 Trim a 138 x 7.5cm (54½ x 3in) strip of butter muslin (cheesecloth) to 6.5cm (2½in) wide. Turn under one long edge only and stitch at the seam-line where Row 1 joins to the sashing. Line up the other long edge and tack (baste) in place through all the layers of fabric.

14 Repeat steps 12 and 13 to finish the bottom of Row 3. Remove the numbered papers from the quilt. The quilt is now ready for the backing to be added.

Adding the backing

1 Measure the width and length of the quilt – it should be approximately 137cm (54in) square. If not, adjust the backing fabric size accordingly. Cut the backing fabric into three 137 x 48cm (54 x 19in) strips.

2 Place one of the strips on the back of the quilt along Row 2. Pin and tack (baste) both long sides in place. With a small running stitch, sew the long edges to the back of the quilt, 1cm (½in) from the raw edges of the backing fabric.

3 On the short sides, with small tacking (basting) stitches, sew to the 1cm (½in) seam allowance.

4 To add the next strip to the back of Row 1, fold under one long edge by 1cm (½in) and press.

5 Lay the folded edge onto the raw edge of the backing fabric at Row 2 so that it just covers the running stitch. Pin and tack (baste) the backing strip in place.

6 With a small ladder stitch, sew along the folded edge to attach the strips together, then tack (baste) the other long edge and two short sides to the seam allowance of Row 1, as in step 3.

7 Complete by adding the last strip to the back of the quilt at Row 3 following steps 4–6, but this time place the folded edge so that it covers the raw edge and running stitches along the bottom of Row 2. Trim any excess fabric from the outside edge of the quilt to the width of the calico (muslin) border sashing. Make sure there is a tacking (basting) line along the 1cm (½in) seam allowance stitched through all the fabric layers.

Quilting

Start in the middle with Block 5 and use the 1cm (½in) masking tape for your guide to quilt around the outside of each block into the sashing, through all the layers of fabric. Quilt in the ditch around each of the small intersecting squares. Work from the centre to the outside edges of the quilt.

Binding

1 Measure the quilt through its centre both horizontally and vertically – this will give you the final measurement for the quilt (mine measured 137cm/54in). The finished width of the binding will be 1cm (½in) to match the width of the quilting. For the sides you will need to cut two calico (muslin) pieces, each 137 x 5.5cm (54 x 2¼in) long.

2 Start with the sides. Pin and tack (baste) the first binding strip to the front edge of the quilt (matching the right side of the fabric strip to the right side of the quilt). Match it to the edge of the quilt and sew 1cm (½in) from the edge through all layers by machine with a medium to long stitch.

3 Fold the binding strip over to the back of the quilt and fold under the excess fabric so that the binding lies flat and is just covering the machine stitching. Hand-stitch this folded edge to the machine stitching on the back of the quilt with either a hemming stitch or a small ladder stitch. Repeat this on the opposite side with the other strip.

4 For the top and bottom edges of the quilt the binding will need to measure the horizontal width plus 2.5cm (1in) to allow for neatening the ends on the corners of the quilt.

5 Cut and add the first of the strips in the same way but remember to allow 1cm (½in) of excess binding to overlap at each end along the top of the quilt before stitching the strip to the front of the quilt as before.

6 Fold the binding over to the back of the quilt and fold in the projecting fabric to make a neat square corner. Turn it under so that the folded edge is just covering the machine stitching. Pin and tack (baste) in place.

7 Ladder stitch or hem stitch the folded edge to the back of the quilt. Hem stitch the corners. Repeat for the bottom edge. The quilt is now finished. Remove all tacking (basting) stitches.

8 Finally stitch the sixteen buttons, through all the layers, to the centre of each of the small squares.

Finishing tip

Always make a label with your name and the date that your quilt is finished and include any information that you might think is relevant. Stitch the label to the back of your quilt.

Festive Cheer table centre

▶ 58.5cm (23in) DIAMETER

This festive table centre contains Christmas roses, mistletoe, holly, ivy, stars and lots of sparkle – there should always be sparkle! It is perfect to stand a candle or small Christmas tree on. I got my inspiration from a collection of Christmas items including old cards and printed paper napkins. The pattern is repeated four times within the circular shape. I chose to stitch the design with red, green, white and gold threads and to embellish with beads and crystals. I added a star motif in the centre of the piece but this area could be cross-hatch quilted if you prefer. The outside edge is turned under and neatened – it makes a nice flat edge, eliminating the need for piping cord or binding.

You will need

- One 70cm (26in) square of white quilters' calico (muslin) for the front of the table centre
- One 70cm (26in) square of backing fabric (I have used a white on white print for this)
- Two 70cm (26in) square pieces of butter muslin (cheesecloth)
- Two 70cm (26in) square pieces of 2oz (57g) Thermore wadding (batting) – although this is a slightly flat wadding (batting), it still retains the 'bounce' or 'loft' required to make the techniques successful
- One skein of quilting wool
- A small bag of toy filler (or scraps of teased-out polyester wadding/batting)
- Machine sewing thread in a variety of colours, including metallic for sewing the design
- Machine sewing thread in ivory, gold and variegated for quilting
- Tacking (basting) thread in a pale blue or pink
- 5mm (¼in) reel of low-tack, masking tape
- A variety of small beads, I used:
  3mm (⅛in) gold
  2mm (¹⁄₁₆in) pale green
  4mm (³⁄₁₆in) transparent crystal facetted beads
  4mm (³⁄₁₆in) blue-green metallic finish beads
  5mm (¼in) gold metallic star-shaped beads
  10mm (½in) and 15mm (²⁄₃in) silver stars
  A small quantity of 3mm (⅛in), 4mm (³⁄₁₆in) and 5mm (¼in) Chinese and Swarovski crystals, both hot- and cold-fix
- Needles
- Stuffing tool
- HB pencil
- A hot-fix tool or a travel iron, and cold-fix appliqué glue

The raised surface is covered with quilting and embellishments – this is a purely decorative piece of work.

Three-dimensional quilting

Template 1A, see also full-size pull-out template

You will first need to make the outer circle from four identical curved pieces using Template 1A, which will need to be traced and carefully pieced together on the calico (muslin). The centre of the project is circular and symmetrical: use Template 1B.

1 Fold the pre-cut square of calico (muslin) in half, then in half again to make four squares. Press very lightly and open out. Tack (baste) with a pale blue thread along the fold lines to quarter the fabric. Secure the design to a flat surface and place the calico (muslin) directly on top of the design. Align the tacking (basting) on one quarter of the fabric with the straight edges of Template 1A, so that the inner curve of the template is towards the centrepoint of the calico (muslin). Use a ruler and check that the outer edge of Template 1A is 28cm (11in) from the centre of the fabric in each direction. Draw the inner and outer curved edges only onto the calico (muslin). Carefully move the calico (muslin) to the adjacent quarter and align the template as before. Repeat for the remaining quarters – you should now have a completed circular shape.

2 Repeat the process and now draw the design into each quarter of the calico (muslin). Secure Template 1B and trace the star centre circle, or leave blank if you want to cross-hatch. Remove the paper design.

3 Tack (baste) one piece of butter muslin (cheesecloth) to the back of the fabric with a 2.5cm (1in) grid and add a final row of tacking (basting) to the outer edge of the design 1cm (½in) away from the perimeter edges of the pattern. Also tack (baste) the outer edge of the square to hold all the fabrics in place. Backstitch the mistletoe and berries, all the holly berries, the star and heart shapes, the centres of the hellebore flowers, sepals and stems, and the outer double star shape on Template 1B. For all the hellebore flower petals, first backstitch with white or pale grey threads then whip stitch with white metallic thread.

4 Next add running stitch: stitch the holly leaves and inner and outer ivy leaf shapes, the double lines on the oval leaf veins, and the inner shape of the double star on Template 1B. The oval leaves were first stitched with running stitch then whip stitched with metallic green thread. The

fern shapes, holly and ivy veins, straight lines on the inner petals of the hellebores, and cow parsley are all left as pencil lines until the quilting stage. Also leave the star designs in the centre circle. If you want to, refer to the finished piece on pages 102–103 for colour inspiration.

5 Use Template 2 to add the extra lines where indicated on the outer band; use Template 1B for the centre circle. Use the masking tape to create the two 5mm (¼in) channels around the centre circle and the three channels around the outer circle. You can carefully bend the tape around the curved shapes where necessary. Sew all the extra lines with running stitch. Look at the guide and whip stitch all the hellebore petals with white

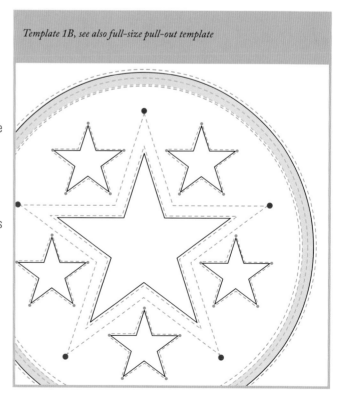

Template 1B, see also full-size pull-out template

100

Template 2

Whip stitch
around all the
hellebore flowers.

Whip stitch
around the leaves.

Template 3

and the outside edge of the oval leaves with green. Remove all the tacking (basting) stitches from the work, leaving only those that are on the outside edge of the pattern. Press both sides of the work. Cover the stitching with a calico (muslin) fabric to protect the metallic threads when ironing.

6 Turn the work to the back and stuff only the pink areas shown on Template 2. Be careful not to over-stuff each of the larger shapes. Stitch the veins into the surface of the holly leaves after stuffing with running stitch.

7 To cord, refer to the green areas shown on Template 2. Start with the channels surrounding the stuffed shapes in the ivy leaves, and then thread the star shapes, remembering to leave very small loops where the design changes direction. Thread the mistletoe with wool and double it where the leaf is wider. Thread any very small shape that would be difficult to stuff – the narrow centres, calyx and stems on the hellebore flowers. Also the narrow veins on the oval leaves. Finally thread the centre circles, starting with the inner channel. If possible, use a longer piece of wool but be very careful when pulling it in and out of the channels so that it does not part – or thread it in two halves. Then thread the outside channels on the circle. Again, use longer wool or thread in two halves. Make sure the circles are kept flat and not pulled into gathers.

8 Pin and tack (baste) the two pieces of wadding (batting) – to form a double layer – and then add the butter muslin (cheesecloth) to the back of the runner with grid tacking (basting) as before. Tack all the layers together.

9 Quilt using templates 3 and 1B, with the star motif or cross-hatch quilt instead. Start in the centre with the star motif. Stitch all the stars with a metallic thread. Echo the centre star shape with ivory cotton thread and all around the circle, both sides of the channels. Next, quilt inside and outside the outer band, either side of the treble channel that forms the edge of the work. For the detail in the decorative band, use the ivory-coloured thread to quilt around all the flowers, berries and leaf shapes. Quilt the ivy veins just into the surface of the wadding (batting). Also quilt the lines on the hellebore petals.

10 Quilt all the remaining pencil lines and shapes with metallic threads – I backstitch quilted the fern and cow parsley shapes with gold; the small stars were quilted with backstitch and the large stars with running stitch. Quilt through all the layers 1cm (½in) away from the last quilted line on the outer edge of the circle close to the 1cm (½in) tacking (basting) line. Carefully remove all the tacking (basting) threads.

101

Making up

1 Mark with pencil a line 2cm (¾in) away from the previous quilting all around the outside edge of the circle. Cut away on this line and discard the excess calico (muslin). Fold back the 2cm (¾in) of calico (muslin) onto the front of the work and pin in place to reveal the remaining layers.

2 Carefully cut away the butter muslin (cheesecloth) and wadding (batting) from the back of the work – 2mm (¹/₁₆in) away from the quilting line, leaving the calico (muslin) intact. Remove the pins and fold the calico (muslin) to the back of the work on the quilting line.

3 Pin to the back of the work and with herringbone or very small tacking (basting), stitch in place ensuring that the stitches are not visible from the right side.

4 Next add all the embellishments – shown in blue on Template 3 – stitch any beads on first, then hot-fix and finally cold-fix the crystals in place, following the maker's instructions. Leave to cure overnight. Always test the crystals on a spare piece of fabric and check the drying time before embarking on the table centre as mistakes cannot be rectified once the stones are in place.

5 To finish, lay the backing fabric right side down on a flat surface. Place the table centre on top – use this as a pattern and cut out the backing fabric, making it the same size as the table centre. Pin the backing fabric to the wrong side of the table centre to prevent the material from slipping. Turn under the raw edge of the backing fabric and carefully pin it in place all around 5mm (¼in) from the outer edge of the work. Ladder stitch to the back of the work with small stitches. You will find that the quilting has pulled the work in slightly and it now measures approximately 58.5cm (23in) in diameter.

The image below shows most of the design repeat with all the quilting and embellishments completed.

The completed table centre: the turned edge makes a flat, neat finish.

Candle tip

If you want to place a lit candle on top, remember to ensure that it is fixed to a suitable base before standing it on the table centre – you do not want hot wax to burn or spoil the fabric. Never leave candles unattended and where possible use battery-operated flickering candles.

The centre shows the quilted stars with flat back crystals in place. The centre is left flat so that decorations can be placed on it without toppling over.

Winter Snow table runner

▶ 209 x 104cm (82 x 41in) AT ITS WIDEST POINT

I just love Christmas! As far back as I can remember, it has been a magical time of year in our family – I can remember my father dragging home what seemed like half a tree and then having to manipulate it into the front room. He would then set about cutting chunks from the base until it fitted into the corner perfectly with only a tiny space between the tree and the ceiling! These days, my house is often compared to a Christmas grotto, as I spend about two weeks getting it ready; now I have grandchildren it is even more important to continue these family traditions.

Having been inspired to make a festive table runner, I chose snowflakes and reindeers as the subjects for the design. I chose a blue and white colour scheme to make it a little different from the traditional red and green and then I found some interesting Christmas fabrics that I just had to use. The addition of crystal embellishment was too much of a temptation to ignore.

I like my table runner designs to be a little unusual and so decided to make this one with a shaped edge. As with much of my work, it grew as the design progressed. There are seven blocks to this runner, two of which are mirror imaged – so be careful when you draw them out – and follow the guidelines for the stitching, cording, stuffing and quilting. The embellishment is added at the very end and is optional. You could make a set of Christmas pillows if you do not want the table runner – or it can be used as a wall hanging if you prefer.

Read through the instructions before you begin and familiarise yourself with the shapes and how the work is made up into the table runner. Depending on how you sew, you might have to make little adjustments at the making up stage.

You will need

Sizes based on a 112cm (44in) fabric width unless otherwise stated

- 1m (1¼ yds) of white quilters' calico (muslin) for the snowflake blocks
- 3.5m (4 yds) butter muslin (cheesecloth)
- 2.25m (2½ yds) of backing fabric
- 60cm (23¾in) fabric for binding
- 4m (4½ yds) of 2oz (57g) Thermore wadding (batting), 1m (1¼ yds) wide: this is flatter but still retains the 'bounce' or 'loft' required to make this technique successful. Do not be tempted to use cotton or blanket types of wadding (batting) – they have insufficient 'loft' or 'bounce' in the fibres
- 50cm (20in) of each of the following:
  Blue and white sparkle fabric (A)
  Grey with white snowballs fabric (B)
  Blue and white fabric with printed festive words (C)
  Blue and white spot fabric (D)
- 1m (1¼ yds) plain blue fabric for stag blocks and for striped panels (E)
- Two skeins of quilting wool
- Bag of toy filler (or scraps of polyester wadding/batting)
- Machine sewing thread in matching colours to your fabrics, including metallic thread for stitching the design, blue perlé embroidery thread and variegated thread in mid-grey
- One skein of white stranded embroidery cotton
- Machine sewing thread in ivory, silver and blue for quilting
- Tacking (basting) thread in a pale green or pink colour
- A variety of flower-shaped crystal beads: I used 5mm (¼in) and 1cm (½in) sizes in iridescent colours
- A small quantity of clear 3mm (⅛in), 4mm (³⁄₁₆in) and 5mm (¼in) Chinese crystals – (some Swarovski) – both hot- and cold-fix in faceted shapes
- Four 15mm (²⁄₃in) silver sew-on stars
- Needles
- Stuffing tool
- HB pencil
- Hot-fix tool or a travel iron
- Cold-fix appliqué glue

The layout

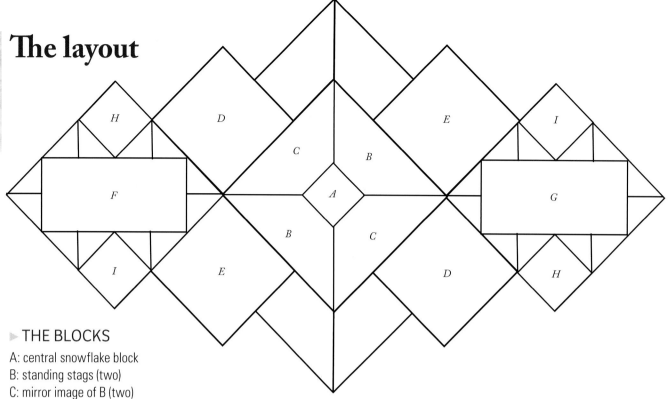

▶ THE BLOCKS

A: central snowflake block
B: standing stags (two)
C: mirror image of B (two)
D: large snowflake (two)
E: large snowflake (two)
F: running stags
G: mirror image of F
H: small snowflake (two)
I: small snowflake (two)

The remaining shapes are made from quilt-as-you-go strips of Christmas fabric.

*The table runner is made up from a variety of blocks –
see the diagram above for block placements.*

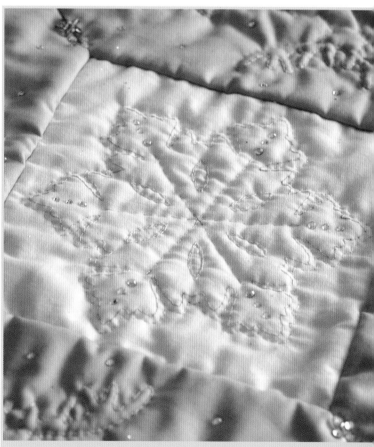

*Block A: this snowflake is kept as flat as possible so that you can stand items on
the middle of the runner without them toppling over.*

Three-dimensional quilting

Start the table runner by making the stag and snowflake blocks: select the patterns that you will need and cut out the fabrics for each of these blocks before you start to stitch. Unless stated otherwise, a 1cm (½in) seam allowance will be used – this will allow for any trimming that might be required later.

▶ BLOCK A: CENTRE SNOWFLAKE

1 First, cut a 20cm (8in) square from the white calico (muslin), two 20cm (8in) squares of butter muslin (cheesecloth) and one 20cm (8in) piece of wadding (batting).

2 Using Template 1, very lightly draw out the border 1cm (½in) inside the calico (muslin) square to make a new 18cm (7in) square. Carefully trace the snowflake within this square – the top of the design should line up with one of the corners of the calico (muslin) – the design is what is known as 'on point'. Remove the paper pattern.

3 Tack (baste) one piece of butter muslin (cheesecloth) to the back of the design – this is used as a support fabric only for this block, to keep the snowflake the same weight as the other blocks and to make the stitching easier. Tack (baste) all around the square with small stitches.

4 Stitch the outline of the design with backstitch in variegated grey sewing machine thread. Backstitch the oval shapes with a pale blue thread. Press the work on both sides.

5 Add the wadding (batting) and second piece of butter muslin (cheesecloth) to the back of the work and tack (baste) the layers together. This block is not stuffed or corded.

6 Using silver thread, quilt through all the layers starting with the central radiating lines. Refer to Template 2. Double stitch the centres to make a star shape where the lines cross over.

7 Quilt around the ovals with whip stitch quilting using an iridescent thread. Echo quilt around the outside of the snowflake 3mm (¹/₈in) away from the outline. Leave the eighteen dots at the points of the snowflake – these indicate where you will attach your crystals at the final stage.

8 Remove all the tacking (basting) stitches from the centre of the work but leave them in the seam allowance. Write the template letter on a small piece of paper and pin it to the top centre of the block with a safety pin. Put the block to one side.

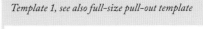
Template 1, see also full-size pull-out template

Top

Template 2

▶ BLOCKS B AND C: STANDING STAGS, MAKE TWO OF EACH

1 Cut a piece of blue fabric to 20 x 48.5cm (8 x 19in). Also cut two pieces of butter muslin (cheesecloth) and one piece of wadding (batting) to the same size.

2 Trace the trapezium shape and the stags from Template 1 onto the blue fabric. Trace the plants at either side of the stags and mark with a dot the placing for the embellishments: the half stars and all the small circles. Remove the paper template. Put one piece of butter muslin (cheesecloth) on the back of the blue fabric and tack (baste) the pieces together in a grid formation – also tack (baste) the seam allowance.

3 Stitch the stags with backstitch using two strands of white embroidery thread. Remove the tacking (basting) from the stitched areas. Press the work on both sides.

4 Fill the stag bodies as shown on Template 2: the pink areas should be stuffed, and where the shapes are too narrow to stuff – the legs and antlers, shown in green – thread with wool, burying one end into the stuffing, leaving a small tail at the other end.

5 Add the wadding (batting) and second butter muslin (cheesecloth) layer to the back of the work and tack (baste) the layers together.

6 With matching blue sewing thread, quilt around the stags close to the white stitching, as shown on Template 2. Use the silver thread to quilt the plant on the right-hand side with running stitch. Whip stitch quilt the leaf veins in silver. Whip stitch quilt the stems with blue sparkle thread. Quilt the plant on the left-hand side in silver running stitch for the leaves and backstitch for the stem. Quilt the remaining fern-shaped plants with fly stitch, use detached chain at the ends of some of the fronds in silver (see page 115). For now, ignore the blue circles on the template: these are where you will apply your embellishments at the final stage.

7 Remove all the tacking (basting) stitches from the centre of the work but leave them in the seam allowance. Write the template letter on a small piece of paper and pin it to the top centre of the block with a safety pin. Put the block to one side.

8 Make a second identical Block B.

9 You will now need to make two of Block C by using the template in reverse. Once your designs are transferred onto your fabric, make them in exactly the same way as Block B.

Template 1, see also full-size pull-out template

Template 2

108

Template 1, see also full-size pull-out template

Template 2

Template 3

▶ BLOCK D: LARGE SNOWFLAKE, MAKE TWO

1 Cut a 38cm (15in) square from white calico (muslin). Also cut two squares of butter muslin (cheesecloth) and one square of wadding (batting) to the same size. Very lightly draw a 32cm (12½in) square within the calico (muslin). Carefully trace the snowflake pattern 'on point', lining up the top of the design with a corner.

2 Tack (baste) one of the butter muslin (cheesecloth) squares to the back of the work in a grid formation and then tack (baste) all around the square in the seam allowance line with small stitches. Start from the centre of the design and work towards the outside. Backstitch the first two hexagon shapes in the centre of the snowflake with grey sewing thread. Change to the blue thread and backstitch the third hexagon and its radiating lines that extend out to the circle shapes. Next use the variegated perlé thread and with running stitch sew around the inner diamond shapes then backstitch the circles and the double line above them. With running stitch sew around the remaining main 'branches' and the 'V' shape found close to the smaller outer circle. With blue thread, backstitch the outside edges of the diamonds that form a star shape. Use pale grey sewing thread and backstitch both sides of the half moon shapes, then with running stitch sew the petal shaped curves that are inside of each diamond. Finally backstitch the smaller outer circles with the grey thread. Do not stitch the 'leaves' that emerge from the branches – these will be completed later. Remove the tacking (basting) threads and press the work on both sides.

3 Refer to Template 2 for the stuffing and cording. Stuff the circles, the centre of the hexagon and the petal shapes, shown in pink. Thread all the areas shown in green: cord the double lines with wool, remembering to leave very small loops at the points and short tails where you start and finish a channel. Thread the V-shaped 'branches'.

4 Add the wadding (batting) and second butter muslin (cheesecloth) squares to the back of the work and tack (baste) the layers together. Refer to Template 3 and quilt only the areas indicated. Start from the centre of the work. With silver thread, quilt around the outside of the corded hexagon shape, then inside the large hexagon keeping close to the original stitching. Next quilt around the outside edge of the diamonds that form the star shape and outside the large circles close to the previous rows of stitching. Echo quilt 2mm (¹⁄₁₆in) away from the outside of the smaller circles. With pale blue sparkle thread quilt around the outside edge of the half moon shapes. Use ivory sewing thread to quilt close to the 'branches' where shown. Change back to the silver thread and stitch just into the surface of the wadding (batting) around each of the 'leaves' on either side of the 'branches' with small running stitches (see the close-up, below).

5 For now, ignore the blue marks on the template: these are where you will apply your embellishments at the final stage. Remove all the tacking (basting) stitches from the centre of the work but leave them in the seam allowance. Write the template letter on a small piece of paper and pin it to the top centre of the block with a safety pin. Put the work to one side. Make a second identical Block D snowflake.

Template 3: close-up

Top

Template 1, see also full-size pull-out template

Template 2

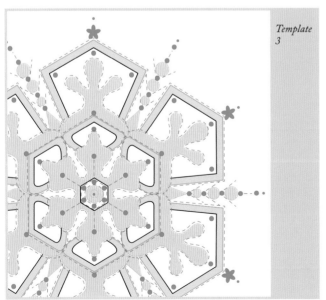

Template 3

▶ BLOCK E: LARGE SNOWFLAKE, MAKE TWO

1 Cut a 38cm (15in) square from the white calico (muslin). Also cut two squares of butter muslin (cheesecloth) and one square of wadding (batting) to the same size. Very lightly draw a 32cm (12½in) square within the calico (muslin). Carefully trace the snowflake pattern 'on point', lining up the top of the design with a corner as before.

2 Tack (baste) one of the butter muslin (cheesecloth) squares to the back of the work in a grid formation and then tack (baste) all around the square in the seam allowance line with small stitches. Start from the centre of the design and work towards the outside. With blue sewing thread, backstitch the hexagon shape close to the centre of the snowflake. Change to the variegated perlé thread and stitch the circle at the centre of the design with running stitch. Next backstitch around the flower shape. Change to the grey thread and backstitch the outside edge of the pointed oval shape found at the end of each flower petal and with running stitch sew the inside edge of this shape. Use the matt finished perlé thread to backstitch the curving swirly line and sew with running stitch the inside of the four sided shape that resembles a pentagon. Change to the blue sewing thread and backstitch the outside of this shape. With the grey thread backstitch the pointed shape and three circles found between the six pentagon shapes. Remove the tacking (basting) threads then press the work on both sides.

3 Refer to Template 2 for the stuffing and cording. Stuff all the areas shown in pink. Cord all the areas shown in green: thread with wool, remembering to leave small loops at the points and short tails where you start and finish a channel.

4 Add the wadding (batting) and second butter muslin (cheesecloth) squares to the back of the work and tack (baste) the layers together.

5 Start from the centre of the work. With silver thread, quilt around the outside of the centre circle and then inside of the hexagon close to the original stitching. Use the ivory sewing thread to quilt around the outside of the flower and the swirly shape, close to the original stitching. Change back to the silver thread and quilt around the outside of the pointed oval shape and then echo quilt 2mm (¹/₁₆in) away from the outside edge of the pentagon shapes. With blue sparkle thread whip stitch quilt around the outside edge of the pointed shapes and three circles. Finally quilt with silver thread and backstitch the radiating lines that are found emerging from the three circles on the outside edge of the snowflake.

6 For now, ignore the blue marks on the template: these are where you will apply your embellishments at the final stage.

7 Remove all the tacking (basting) stitches from the centre of the work but leave them in the seam allowance. Write the template letter on a small piece of paper and pin it to the top centre of the block with a safety pin. Put the work to one side. Make a second identical Block E snowflake.

BLOCKS F AND G: RUNNING STAGS, MAKE TWO OF EACH

Template 1, see also full-size pull-out template

Template 2

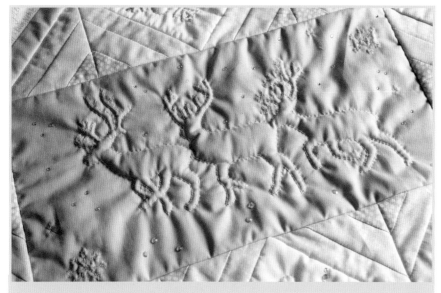

Block G is the mirror image of Block F. The stags appear to be running towards the herd that has gathered in the centre.

1 Cut a piece of blue fabric to 26.5 x 45.5cm (10½ x 18in). Also cut two pieces of butter muslin (cheesecloth) and one piece of wadding (batting) to the same size. Trace the rectangle and the stags from Template 1 centrally onto it. Trace the snowflakes at either side of the stags and mark with a dot the placing for the embellishments. Remove the paper template.

2 Put one piece of butter muslin (cheesecloth) on the back of the blue fabric and tack (baste) together in a grid formation. Also tack (baste) the seam allowance.

3 Stitch the stags with backstitch using two strands of white embroidery thread. Remove the tacking (basting) from the stitched areas. Press the work on both sides.

4 Fill the stag bodies as shown on Template 2: the pink areas should be stuffed, and where the shapes are too narrow to stuff – the legs and antlers, shown in green – thread with wool, burying one end into the stuffing and leave a small tail at the other end.

5 Add the wadding (batting) and second butter muslin (cheesecloth) squares to the back of the work and tack (baste) the layers together.

6 With matching blue sewing thread, quilt around the stags close to the white stitching as shown on Template 2. Quilt the small snowflakes with silver double cross stitch star (see page 25). Quilt the larger snowflakes with fly stitch in silver thread and add straight stitches to the connecting lines. For now, ignore the blue circles on the template: these are where you will apply your embellishments at the final stage.

7 Remove all the tacking (basting) stitches from the centre of the work but leave them in the seam allowance. Write the template letter on a small piece of paper and pin it to the top centre of the block with a safety pin. Put the work to one side. Make a second identical Block F.

8 You will now need to make two of Block G by using the templates in reverse. Once your design is transferred onto your fabric, make the blocks in exactly the same way as for Block F.

111

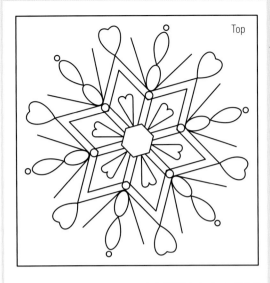

▶ BLOCK H: SMALL SNOWFLAKE, MAKE TWO

1 Cut a 20cm (8in) square from white calico (muslin). Also cut two squares of butter muslin (cheesecloth) and one square of wadding (batting) to the same size. Very lightly draw a 15cm (6in) square within the calico (muslin). Carefully trace the snowflake pattern 'on point', lining up the top of the design with a corner, as before. Remove the paper template.

2 Tack (baste) one of the butter muslin (cheesecloth) squares to the back of the work in a grid formation and then tack (baste) all around the square in the seam allowance line with small stitches. Backstitch the centre hexagon shape with blue perlé thread. Create the inner diamond shapes in running stitch and the outer diamond shapes in backstitch. I have used a perlé thread variegated from pale to mid-blue, which has a sheen finish. The hearts are backstitched in pale blue sewing thread and the oval and teardrop shapes are backstitched in grey. Remove the tacking (basting) stitches from the stitched area. Press on both sides of the work.

3 Stuff the hexagon centre, the heart and teardrop ovals, as shown in pink. These are very small shapes so do not overstuff them. Cord the areas shown in green. Thread the double lines with wool, remembering to leave very small loops at the points and short tails where you start and finish.

Template 2

4 Add the wadding (batting) and second butter muslin (cheesecloth) squares to the back of the work and tack (baste) the layers together.

5 Quilt around the hexagon and the outside of the star shape with ivory sewing thread as close to the previous stitching as possible. Using silver thread, quilt the inner heart shapes, outer heart shapes, teardrops and ovals. Finally backstitch the radiating lines with the silver thread.

6 For now, ignore the blue marks on the template: these are where you will apply your embellishments at the final stage.

7 Remove all the tacking (basting) stitches from the centre of the work but leave them in the seam allowance. Write the template letter on a small piece of paper and pin it to the top centre of the block with a safety pin. Put the work to one side. Make a second identical Block H snowflake.

Template 3

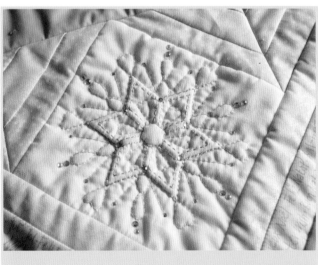

Block H snowflake, complete with embellishments.

▶ BLOCK I: SMALL SNOWFLAKE, MAKE TWO

1 Follow step 1 on page 112 to cut and prepare your fabrics and trace off your template as for Block H.

2 Tack (baste) one of the butter muslin (cheesecloth) squares to the back of the work in a grid formation and then tack (baste) all around the square in the seam allowance line with small stitches.

3 Stitch the inner star shape with running stitch and the outer star shape in backstitch using the variegated perlé thread. Backstitch the circles in pale blue sewing thread and the connecting double lines with the matt finished perlé thread. Stitch the double V-shaped lines with backstitch in grey. Remove the tacking (basting) stitches from the stitched areas. Press the work on both sides.

4 Stuff the circles shown in pink on Template 2. Cord the areas shown in green. Thread all the double lines with wool, remembering to leave very small loops at the points and short tails where you start and finish a channel. Thread the V-shapes.

5 Add the wadding (batting) and second butter muslin (cheesecloth) squares to the back of the work and tack (baste) the layers together.

6 Refer to Template 3 for quilting. With the silver thread, quilt the diamonds and connecting lines in the centre of the star with whip stitch quilting. Use the ivory thread to quilt close to the outside of the star shape and the outside of the connecting lines. Change to the silver thread and quilt around the outside of the circles and the V-shapes.

7 For now, ignore the blue marks on the template: these are where you will apply your embellishments at the final stage.

8 Remove all the tacking (basting) stitches from the centre of the work but leave them in the seam allowance. Write the template letter on a small piece of paper and pin it to the top centre of the block with a safety pin. Put the work to one side. Make a second identical Block I snowflake.

Template 1, see also full-size pull-out template

Top

Template 2

Block I snowflake – all the snowflakes are set on point in the square fabric.

Template 3

113

The striped sections

The striped sections are quilted directly onto a piece of wadding (batting) – they can be stitched by hand, but the technique I have used ('stitch and flip', a variation of quilt-as-you-go) is ideal to sew by machine. Set the machine to a medium to long stitch size and use a jeans, heavy-duty or size 110 needle – if the needle is too fine it will bend and break.

1 Cut four pieces of wadding (batting) to 36 x 18cm (14 x 7in). From each of the Christmas fabrics and the blue fabric, cut two strips, 4cm (1½in) wide, across the width of the fabric. Cut each of these fabrics into 36cm (14in) lengths. Only cut two strips each time – cut more as you need them. Set out the fabrics that will form the stripes that sit next to stag Blocks B and C, and decide the order for stitching them together. I repeated the same blue fabric that I had used for the stags on the outside edge (E) as I felt it gave a better balance to the work. The order I worked in was: E, B, D, C, B, A (see below for reference).

2 Take a strip of wadding (batting) and place your first 4cm (1½in) strip of fabric (A), vertically, right side up on the right-hand edge of the wadding (batting). Pin or tack (baste) in place. Machine stitch the right-hand side to the wadding (batting), 5mm (¼in) from the raw edges down the length of the fabric strip.

3 Start from the top again and put a second strip of fabric (B) – wrong side up – on top of the first fabric (A). Pin or tack (baste) into place. Machine through all of the layers on the left-hand side of the strip as it faces you, with a 5mm (¼in) seam allowance. Fold fabric B over towards the left, so that the right side of the fabric is uppermost, and thumb press the seam open revealing that fabric A is stitched on both edges. Pin fabric B to keep it flat.

4 Take a third strip (C) and place this right side down on top of fabric B and repeat the process as before, stitching down and then opening out. Continue in this way until the wadding (batting) is covered with six strips of your chosen fabric. Machine the left-hand edge of the sixth fabric to the wadding (batting) to hold the strip in place. You will see that the strips are self-neatening and give the appearance of stitch in the ditch quilting from the front without the stitching being visible. By starting at the top each time, you will ensure that the strips of fabric remain flat and that the wadding (batting) does not start to twist and distort. Repeat this on all four pieces of wadding (batting) – do not trim any excess wadding (batting) from the edge of the sixth fabric. Place the four completed strips to one side.

5 You will need to create a second set of stripes for either end of the runner to surround stag Blocks F and G. You will cut these strips into triangles. I have used fabrics C, B and E. Cut four strips 4cm (1½in) wide across the width of the fabric. Cut four pieces of wadding (batting) to 10 x 112cm (4 x 44in).

6 Start with fabric C and carefully pin and stitch this to the edge of a wadding (batting) piece as before. Stitch and flip the remaining two strips in place. Be careful not to allow these longer pieces of fabric to be stretched onto the wadding (batting). Pin each one in place prior to stitching. Make four identical strips in total.

7 Use the template provided on the pull-out template to carefully cut out the triangles. The long edge should be placed on fabric C: it will become the outside edge of the block. You will need twelve identical triangles to make up each stag block: twenty-four in total. Leftover striped fabrics should be set apart from those cut using the template.

Ensure that the seam-line between stag Blocks B and C continues down between the striped pieces in a straight, neat join.

Unit 1

1 As the first stage in construction you will need to join the stag and small snowflake blocks into three 'units'. Start by making the central Unit 1 (shown right). Cut out the four stag Blocks B and C, 1cm (½in) outside the tacked (basted) seam allowance. This unit should be made with care as it is an odd shape. Lay the blocks out in front of you so they form a square.

2 With a 1cm (½in) seam allowance, join one Block C to one Block B along the diagonal seam, right sides together. Start at the beginning of the outside edge and stitch towards the centre, stopping at the seam allowance: this should be 1cm (½in) from the end of the fabric. Repeat with the other two blocks.

3 Join these two V-shaped sections together to form the square. Tack (baste) them together first with small stitches to ensure you have joined them in the correct order: the stags should mirror image each other all around the square. Machine stitch the diagonal joins together with a medium-length stitch.

4 From the wrong side, trim away the wadding (batting) and butter muslin (cheesecloth) close to the stitched line along the seam allowance. This will reduce the bulk and help the seams to lie flat. Thumb press the seam allowance open flat and hand-stitch this to the back of the blocks with running stitch catching into the wadding (batting), but not allowing any stitches to show through to the front of the work. Neaten each of the seams in the same way.

5 Fold each edge of the inner square to the back of the work along the seam allowance and tack (baste) through all the layers, 5mm (¼in) from the fold with small stitches.

6 Place Snowflake A underneath the centre opening of the stag blocks, lining up the corners so that the tacked (basted) seam allowance on the snowflake matches the seam allowance of the opening. Check that the centre lies flat. Pin and tack (baste) together, then ladder stitch the stag blocks, along the folded edge, to the snowflake with small invisible stitches. Remove all the tacking (basting) stitches from the front of the stag blocks. If you wish, you could now carefully machine stitch along the ladder stitched line around all four sides of the snowflake to ensure all layers are sewn together.

7 Turn the work to the wrong side. Trim away the excess fabric and wadding (batting) from the seams as before. Trim any excess snowflake fabric to a 1cm (½in) seam allowance. Thumb press the seam allowances away from the centre and stitch to the backing to neaten and flatten.

Pressing warning!

Remember that you will not be able to press this work as this would flatten the raised work and the quilting.

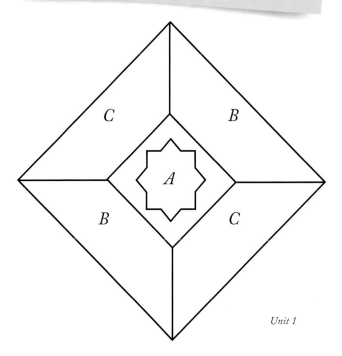

Unit 1

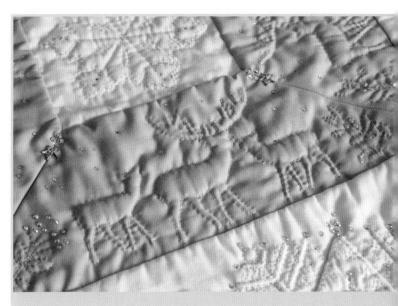

Block C: the simple silhouette of the stags complements the intricate snowflake designs. Block C is the mirror image of Block B.

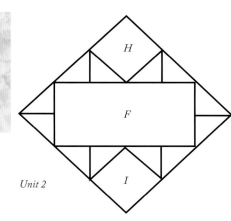

Unit 2

Unit 2

1 For this piece you will need: stag Block F, small snowflakes H and I and twelve striped triangles.

2 With the right sides together, and perfectly matching the stripes, stitch two triangles together from the apex to the outside edge. Thumb press the seam open flat. Repeat this with the remaining triangles to make six new half-square triangle shapes.

3 Set the block out to check that it will be stitched in the correct order, including the position of the new triangles: see left.

4 Start with snowflake I. With the top point of the design pointing up, place one triangle on top of it, so that it covers the right-hand side, right sides facing. Tack (baste), then machine stitch with a 1cm (½in) seam allowance along the top right-hand edge only. Open out and thumb press the seam flat. Trim the excess wadding (batting) from the snowflake, and stitch the seam allowances to the back to neaten.

5 Stitch a second triangle to the other half of the snowflake block, this time stitching only along the top left-hand edge. Open, thumb press, then neaten all the remaining seams. Stitch the triangle edge to the bottom of stag Block F, matching the seam allowances.

6 Repeat this with snowflake H, attaching the triangles to its bottom edge, and stitch to the top of the stag block. Pin and stitch the two remaining half-square triangles to either end of stag Block F to form the square.

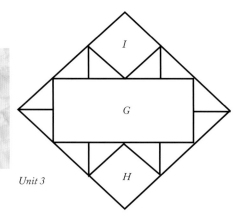

Unit 3

Unit 3

1 Use stag Block G, snowflakes H and I and twelve striped triangles. Set out the block as for Unit 2. Make it up as for Unit 2, above, ensuring that the snowflake blocks are in the correct position.

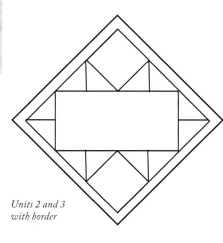

Units 2 and 3 with border

Borders for Units 2 and 3

1 Units 2 and 3 require a border all the way around each square. Cut eight pieces of wadding (batting) to 7 x 53cm (2½ x 21in). Cut eight pieces of fabric B to 4 x 53cm (1½ x 21in). Cut eight pieces of fabric E to 4 x 53cm (1½ x 21in).

2 Using the stitch and flip technique as described on page 114, stitch fabric B, then fabric E to each piece of wadding (batting) with a 5mm (¼in) seam allowance. Border fabric B will be stitched in place, then E becomes the outside edge of the unit.

3 Measure each side of Unit 2 and mark the centre with a pin. Fold a border piece in half to find the centre of its length and mark with a pin. With right sides together, pin and tack (baste) a border to one of the sides, matching the centres – there should be an equal amount of excess border fabric at each end of the side.

4 Stitch in place with a 5mm (¼in) seam allowance, starting and finishing 2.5cm (1in) from either end of the square. Do this for all four sides. Mitre each corner (see page 118). Repeat for Unit 3.

116

Making up

1 Set the three units out as shown below: ensure you position the large snowflake Blocks (D and E), in the correct order, with the wide striped pieces in place. To start, pin, tack (baste) and stitch a striped section to each Block D snowflake with a 1cm (½in) seam allowance. Check that they are stitched the right way round, with fabric E on the long straight edge. Thumb press the seams away from the block and neaten as before.

2 Join a striped section to each Block E snowflake in the same way. Thumb press the seams away from the block and neaten as before.

3 Pin, tack (baste) and stitch the two Block E sections to Unit 1 as shown below, stopping 5cm (2in) from the end of Unit 1 where the striped sections project.

4 Stitching the units together is the final part of the construction – take extra care in aligning the units so they match. Pin, tack (baste), then stitch Units 1 and 2 together from Block E, stopping 5cm (2in) from the end of Unit 1, where the striped section projects. Stitch Unit 3 to Unit 1 in the same way. The striped sections will overlap each other ready to mitre.

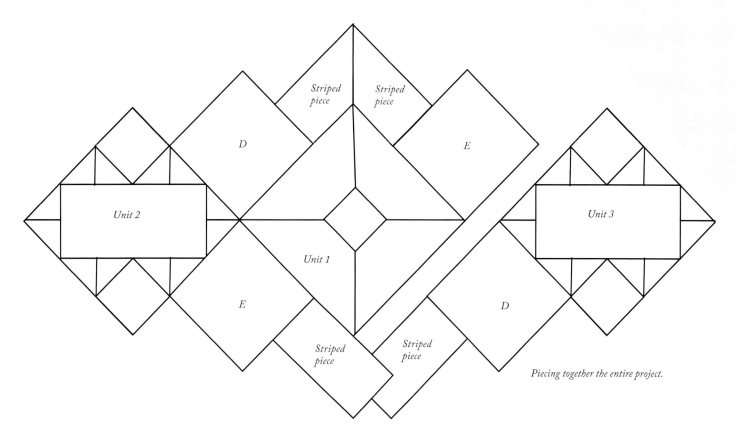

Piecing together the entire project.

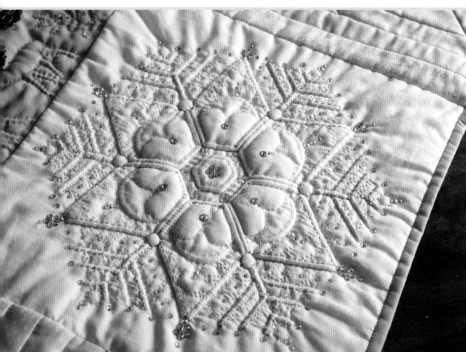

Large snowflake (D) – although this block looks complex, it is easy to make.

To mitre the striped points

1 Start with the two overlapping striped pieces at the bottom of Unit 1. Pin each striped section securely to the Unit 1 block along the 5cm (2in) seam, as if it was about to be stitched, with the same seam allowance as used to stitch the units together. Arrange them so that the right-hand piece is on top.

2 Tuck the end of the right-hand striped section under; keep folding until the stripes match perfectly, and you create a series of chevrons running down the join between the striped pieces.

3 Pin down through all the layers, 5mm (¼in) to the right of this fold.

4 Using a coloured thread, work from the front, with a 1cm (½in) long ladder stitch. Stitch along the fold sewing through the layers to the back of the work. Ensure the striped fabrics match as you go and this will give you a perfect mitre.

5 Remove the pins from the seam allowance to give you easy access for completing the corner. Work from the wrong side – you will see that the ladder stitch has created a perfect tacking (basting) line for stitching the mitre together. Stitch from the outside of the corner towards the centre, stopping at the seam allowance. Cut off the excess striped fabric and leave a 1cm (½in) seam allowance.

6 Finish stitching the unit to the striped section along the seam to each corner. Open and thumb press the mitred seam flat and stitch to neaten.

7 Complete the other mitre in the same way. Neaten all the remaining seams on the runner by stitching them to the back of the work.

8 If you are hand-stitching beads to the table runner for embellishment, sew them on at this stage prior to adding the backing fabric.

Choose fabric colours to match your Christmas décor. Every year I choose a new colour for my festive decorations, and this runner would work well with a blue, silver and white theme.

Backing the table runner

1 With wrong sides together, place the table runner onto the backing fabric. Pin and tack (baste) all the layers together around the outside edge of the table runner, 5mm (¼in) away from the seam allowance. Trim the excess backing fabric away so that it projects slightly from the runner.

2 Quilt by stitching in the ditch through all the layers around centre Block A and around the stag Blocks F and G: this will be sufficient to anchor the backing fabric to the top.

3 With a small running stitch, sew around the perimeter of the work along the seam allowances of the large snowflake blocks and the outside striped section. Trim all the edges 5mm (¼in) away from the running stitch ready for binding. You could use 5mm (¼in) masking tape as a guide to make a more accurate line for cutting away the excess fabric.

Binding and finishing

1 Cut six strips, 4.5cm (1¾in) wide across the width of the binding fabric. The binding can be mitred or have straight corners, whichever you prefer. Twenty edges will require binding. Cut the binding strips a little longer than you need for each edge – it is easier to cut off any excess than trying to piece together fabric in a small space.

2 Start with one of the long sides of Unit 2: cut the first binding fabric the same size as the edge. With right sides together, pin the raw edges of the first strip, matching it to the edge of the table runner. Sew 5mm (¼in) from the edge along the seam allowance, through all layers by machine, with a medium-length stitch.

3 Fold the binding strip over to the back of the quilt, so that the binding fits flat and covers the raw edges. Fold the excess binding under until the folded edge meets the previous row of stitching. Tack (baste) in place. Hand-stitch this folded edge to the back of the runner with either a hemming stitch, or a small ladder stitch.

4 Stitch the next binding strip to the next long edge of Unit 2, but this time leave 1cm (½in) extra fabric projecting from the corner. Fold the extra fabric over the end to the back of the work, turn it in, pin or catch with a stitch to hold it in place. Fold the rest of the binding fabric to the back, turn under, tack (baste) and hand-stitch as before – do not forget to sew the end of each corner with small neat stitches. Continue in this way working around each of the edges of the table runner. You might have to make a couple of adjustments to ensure that the binding fits at the corners. If you wish the corners to look as if they are mitred, when turning under the excess fabric, make a second fold at a right angle to the edge and stitch to the binding that is underneath. You might have to trim away some of the excess material to make a neat corner. This is a bit fiddly to do, but worth the effort.

5 Remove all the visible tacking (basting) stitches from the work, checking every area as you go. Once all the sides are bound the table runner is finished, but if you wish to embellish the stag and snowflake blocks, now is the time to do so.

6 Work with one size or style of crystal at a time, referring back to Template 3 for each of the blocks in turn. While you are working, place your crystals on a piece of felt to prevent them from falling to the floor. If you are using a hot-fix embellishing tool or cold-fix appliqué glue, follow the makers' instructions. Leave the fixing agents to cure overnight before moving the work. Once in place the crystals cannot easily be removed.

Large snowflake Block F.

Safety tip

Take extra care when using the hot-fix tools and keep them away from children – also keep the cold-fix glue out of reach.

Storing tip

When not in use, store the runner on a large cardboard tube. Place it onto a piece of wadding (batting) and roll it around the tube with the right side of the work outside as you wind it on. Make a cotton bag to keep the tube in so it can be put away safe and kept clean for the following year.

Developing designs

With time and practice you will learn which shapes and styles lend themselves well to different raised techniques. Practice any designs you aren't sure about before you commit to using expensive fabrics; what sometimes appears to be a good idea on paper might not work and may well have to be altered during the stitching process, so you must be ready to adapt accordingly.

BE OPEN TO INSPIRATION

My inspiration comes from a variety of sources, much of which is from past and present observations: favourite things, places I love, and the world around me. Sometimes it comes from nature, or from listening to a piece of music, whilst watching a film or visiting an exhibition or museum. It might be from sources as diverse as an image in a magazine, a greetings card, photographs, architecture, wrought iron-work, a doodle created while speaking on the telephone, or a piece of pretty china. I have even found interesting designs embossed into paper kitchen towels. Always be prepared to record information so that it can be used when necessary. Remember, you shouldn't expect to find a design fully formed. Pick and choose elements that you like from different places to create your own unique and exciting designs.

KEEP A NOTEBOOK HANDY

I always keep a small notebook with me so that if I see a shape or something that I find interesting, or read or hear a quote, it is recorded as a quick sketch along with a few written ideas so that I can visit it days, months or even years later to use and adapt into a design suitable for use in my work. Usually when the design I am working on materialises, it triggers further ideas or variations – this process can be hard to stop! Once the initial idea starts to take shape – which can be through a process of several sketches, scribbles or notes – I then plan it out as accurately as possible and scale it up to the finished size. It is changed where necessary – perhaps with elements added or removed – to create a well-proportioned design. I would always advise that you work through this same process with your own designs.

Making a set

If you find or create a design that you really like, why not use it to make a variety of matching items? I used my Moon Flower needlecase pattern (see pages 44–49) to create the items shown right from shades of rose-coloured silk dupion. The fabric was purchased as a themed pack containing six 25cm (10in) squares of silk, which made it very economical.

I chose to include an 18cm (7in) wedding ring pillow to the set in pale pink – I adapted the design slightly and added an extra circle to surround the Moon Flower design for extra interest. The needlecase is quilted on the back with initials and the pincushion is made to the same size. The scissor keeper is designed using half of the Moon Flower pattern and placed diagonally onto the fabric. All of the pieces were quilted in silver thread at the final stage and embellished with hot-fix crystals. Changing the fabric by type or colour will alter the appearance of a design.

Using stencils

Many quilters use stencils. These are either border patterns or single images, and come in a variety of sizes. In my experience, once used they are usually kept just for their original intended purpose, but I want to encourage you to give them another life. Draw out the intended pattern onto paper using a pencil and look at it to see if there are any shapes that can be adapted to the raised work – either for cording, or shapes suitable for stuffing. Draw in the extra double lines that you think will work and also draw in areas that might be stuffed – add to the original pattern if you want or take out parts that will not work. The next stage is to decide which item this could be used for and trace off the new pattern onto a separate piece of paper. If it needs enlarging or reducing, this is the time to change it. Draw it up to its final size and indicate the areas that should be stuffed or filled with parallel corded rows.

To make further use of the stencils, why not combine two or more of them? Again, draw out the patterns and look for areas for cording and stuffing, then proceed to re-draw into the new pattern and size. The pillow shown right was made using two different stencils intended for quilting borders. One is a simple row of squares joined as diamond shapes with a four-petal flower inside each diamond. Outside each diamond there is a second row of lines intended to indicate echo quilting. The other stencil has a pattern of three parallel swirly lines with a loop design to form a corner – a little more of a challenge to use. I drew out the parallel pattern shape first, taking out one of the lines, and joined it up to form a square with a Fleur de Lys shape adapted from the loop in each corner. I then in-filled the centre space by mirror imaging the diamond shapes to form a grid. The echo lines produced an idea that every other row should form concentric squares – it fitted perfectly. To give more variety within the grid pattern, every other flower shape is stuffed. Fortunately, this new pattern did not need to be re-sized and it made a very pleasing design that influenced the bucket bag project.

Here you can see the stencils that were combined, along with the finished pillow. Knot Garden, 46 x 46cm (18 x 18in).

Adapting designs from a stencil

Don't be afraid to adapt a design from a stencil once you have the basic elements in place. Consider how you can further sub-divide shapes with stitching, and where you can add embellishments to give a different feel. To the right you can see three completed items made using variations of one stencil. The 13cm (5in) white calico (muslin) sample, left, could be made into a needlecase, pincushion or framed to hang on the wall. The 23cm (9in) coffee-coloured silk dupion version, centre, that I have named Fleur de Lys, is suitable as a wedding ring pillow. It is stitched and quilted in self colours, then embellished with beads and oval pearls. The 23cm (9in) pale lavender silk dupion wedding ring pillow named Wild Rose becomes a third design. This is stitched in self colour, quilted in silver thread and embellished with various shapes of crystal beads and jewelled cardmakers' split pins.

Using moodboards

It is useful to create a moodboard, especially if you have a theme in mind, or if you are nervous about creating your own designs. I use the term 'moodboard' very loosely – you should work in a way that suits you. It may be that you find it helpful to use a small notice board that you pin a variety of images onto, together with sketches, written thoughts and useful websites. You could add colours, swatches of fabric and threads to this as you find them. Or your moodboard could take the form of a small box in which you can collect a variety of things that relate to a particular idea. It might also be a sketchbook or a ring binder with plastic wallets in which you can store things. There are very few rules to follow – what's important is storing up all the visual stimulation you need to formulate your ideas.

INSPIRATIONS FROM VINTAGE CHINA: SKETCHBOOK PAGE

I have always been interested in vintage china and have been collecting pieces that catch my eye for many years. These can be a good source for design ideas. Inspiration has to spring from somewhere, whether that place is an object, a photograph or the kitchen cupboard.

When I have gathered together inspiration like this, I will photograph or sketch out details taken from the motifs and shapes found in the cups and saucers, then start to draw out the shape that I have in mind. At the bottom left of the moodboard you can see an initial idea for a pillow starting to take shape. Sometimes I start with the finished size for the item; at other times I trace out a couple of patterns, then enlarge them to see how they will look at full size. I usually make several copies and re-trace until I am happy with the outcome. I then make a master copy of the finished piece, which will include all the raised techniques planned out, and also perhaps the colours to be used for the basic stitching and quilting. Sometimes more than one design emerges, so then a series of patterns can be developed.

Until a trial piece is made up, the stitching and quilting ideas might need to be adjusted along the way. What is put down on paper does not always work – the results might need further refinement. Be flexible with the ideas that emerge: a design that starts life as a pillow might eventually end up as a quilt!

Vintage china moodboard taking shape. In the bottom left-hand corner is the sketch being developed from the different sources.

INSPIRATIONS FROM EGYPTIAN ARCHITECTURE: SKETCHBOOK PAGE

I have found Ancient Egyptian artefacts to be a great source of design inspiration for many of my projects. Museum visits are an excellent source of inspiration – several years ago I came across an artefact of a mummified cat that had an interesting interwoven pattern across its surface – I made a quick sketch to remind me of it, with thoughts of possible uses relating to the raised quilting techniques. And several years later, my stylised version of this can be found in the border for the Celtic Lotus wall hanging project (see pages 70–75).

I was also given some photographs of interesting architectural details from a student who had been on holiday in Egypt, so I gathered these together along with some sketches and fabrics in colours that I associate with Egypt. The Nile Lotus bolster pillow in blue silk (bottom right) features several of the patterns found in the photographs, in a rich, luxurious fabric. In addition to this, I thought that a folded patchwork technique was ideal for the ends of the bolster as it reminds me of mummification. The Nile Treasures pillow is another design that has evolved from the top of the column seen in one of the photographs.

Nile Treasures pillow

◀ 51 x 46cm (20 x 18in)

The pillow is developed from photographs depicting Egyptian architectural antiquities. It is made from cream calico (muslin), then stitched with coloured threads in running stitch and backstitch and quilted in cream. This pattern, when made in two halves, could be made into a tea cosy or even a silk handbag.

Nile Lotus bolster pillow

▶ 48cm (19in) LONG WITH A 73cm (29in) CIRCUMFERENCE

Another design based on the photographs. Made in silk dupion, it is stitched in self colour and quilted with self colour and gold thread. It has a ladder-stitched closure. The ends have a piped finish to accentuate the bolster shape and the ends of the bolster are made from the folded 'Lifted Star' design in two shades of silk, as this reminds me of the wrappings of the mummified cat.

123

Be inspired by...

The following pages show quilts that originate from my designs, which have been made by myself and some of my students using the raised three-dimensional quilting techniques.

Symphony 2000

▶ 165 x 160cm (65 x 63in), BY SYLVIA CRITCHER

This is the quilt that evolved, by accident, from the sample shown above right, and started my journey into the development of the traditional techniques. It was here that I became intrigued by the different textures and illusion of layers created across the surface of the work by the use of a single colour and simply using a needle and thread – a modern twist on whole cloth quilting.

The centre panel of this quilt is made from a standard width of fabric – 112cm (44in) – and is 1m (39in) in length. The border is made in four pieces and joined together with mitred corners that utilise the corner motif to hide the join and give the impression that the quilt is made from one piece of cloth. Using the masking tape to act as a guide for stitching the channels occurred to me during the creation of this design, as I wanted to incorporate *le boutis* work but did not want to have the channels quite so narrow. So far it has taken over 400 hours to make. It will – eventually – have its final 46cm (18in) border added.

There are many traditional North Country and Welsh whole cloth quilting designs available but I wanted to select a less well known shape to use for my sample. I chose the paisley motif. The sample was made on plain cream fabric as I had this to hand and it was not until I added the wadding (batting) to the backing and decided to quilt around the shapes and include the knotting that I realised the potential for combining the Italian, trapunto and le boutis *quilting.*

These two enlarged and adapted paisley motifs echo some of those found in the centre panel and are mirror imaged around the outer border.

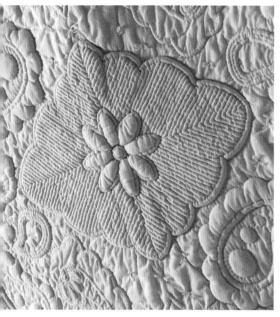

This is the very centre of the quilt. This was the first idea for mirror imaging the sample – the chevron-shaped channels made it possible to easily add a change of direction to the design. At the final quilting stage, stitching around the central flower and only on the outside of the channel motif gives the illusion of the shape being applied to the quilt surface.

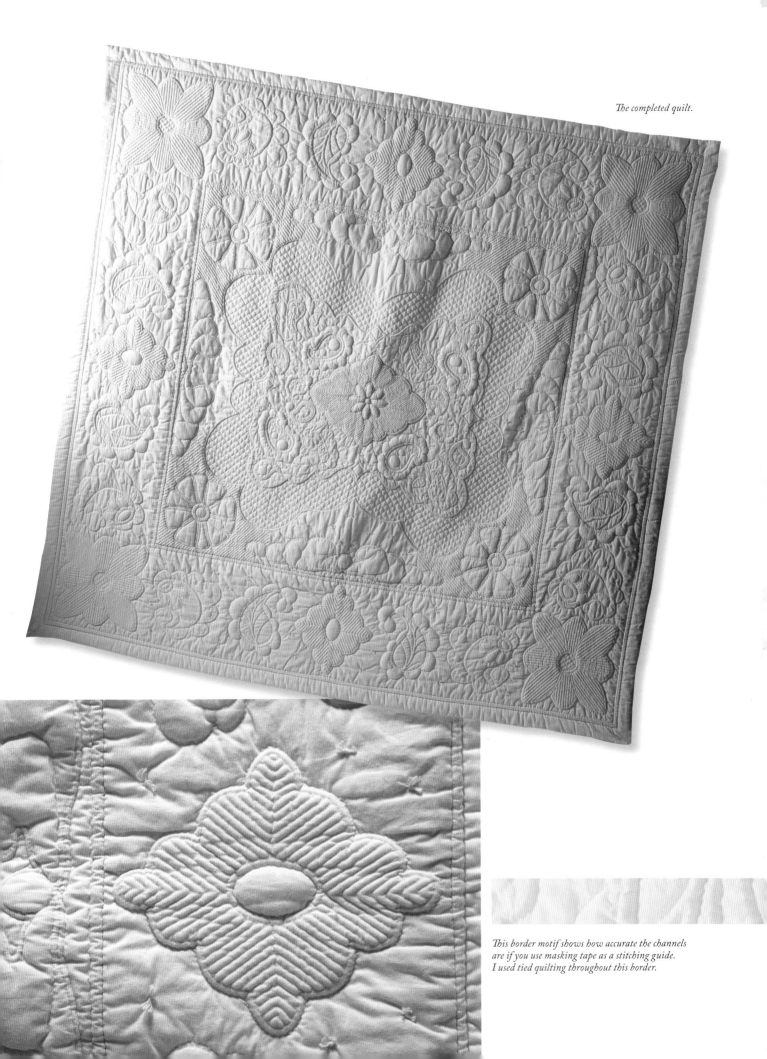

The completed quilt.

This border motif shows how accurate the channels are if you use masking tape as a stitching guide. I used tied quilting throughout this border.

Flora Portamento - Sweet Lavender

▶ 135 x 242cm (53 x 95in),
BY CHRISTINE PARKER

Christine used my 'Flora Portamento' quilt pattern to make this attractive quilt for her sister who is blind. The high relief and tactile surface within the design will enable her to 'see' the pattern through touch. She adores lavender flowers and so this was Christine's obvious colour choice for the fabrics that were chosen. Eighteen blocks, each approximately 43cm (17in) square, were used to make the quilt. It is hand-stitched, hand-quilted and machine-pieced.

The simple border with a bound edge is all that is needed to finish this quilt.

Here, the two 15.25cm (6in) square calico (muslin) centres show off
the two different designs used for the corded and stuffed work. These
alternate across the quilt and are surrounded by pretty printed cotton
fabrics that encompass the range of colours found in lavender plants.
The centres are stitched with running stitch, backstitch and fly stitch.
Stitch in the ditch and echo quilting complement the design.

127

Spanish Roses

▶ 183 x 183cm (72 x 72in), BY BARBARA COX

On my first visit as a tutor at The Spanish Experience in Valencia, Spain, I was asked if I could design a quilt for a group of quilters who had previously enjoyed a one-day course with me. A nine-block quilt-as-you-go quilt seemed ideal, as each person could complete one block during the week-long course, and at the end they could group all their work together to gain an insight into the finished piece. The inspiration for the design came from a Victorian pitcher and ewer that I had been wanting to use in a design for some time – these gave rise to this rose quilt. I used running stitch and backstitch with coloured cotton and polyester threads for the main design, then quilted with white cotton thread – to match the white calico (muslin) fabric. Barbara managed to make two blocks during the week and kept in touch with me afterwards to complete the work – she also added the 25cm (10in) border.

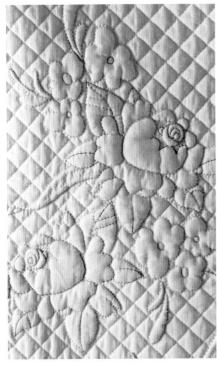

This is one of the two rose blocks that are found either side of the central block. 2cm (¾in) cross-hatch diagonal quilting covers the centre of the quilt, with matching diagonal quilting in the borders.

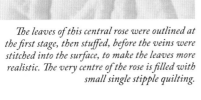

The leaves of this central rose were outlined at the first stage, then stuffed, before the veins were stitched into the surface, to make the leaves more realistic. The very centre of the rose is filled with small single stipple quilting.

Big stitch double stipple quilting surrounds the heart shape on one of the corner pieces. The rose petals are padded in various thicknesses to make more of the three-dimensional flower.

Roses and Butterflies

▶ 2 x 2m (78 x 78in), BY JEAN WITHERICK

Jean used my pillow pattern 'Roses all the Way' as the starting point and centrepiece for this white calico (muslin) quilt. Together we then adapted it to create this beautiful design, which gives the feeling of summer. The trellis design, from the original pattern, repeats throughout to give added structure and is used for the border on the outer edges. The centre panel has a very narrow delicate plain pink border, which is repeated for the bound edge. Cream-coloured thread has been used throughout for the final quilting.

The trellis border shows the background has been 'tied' using clusters of transparent beads. Beads have been used for the centres of the small backstitched flowers and leaves. The small flowers are embellished throughout.

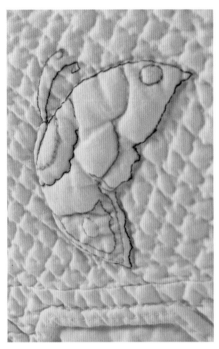

All the butterflies have been stitched with backstitch and split stitch to create definition.

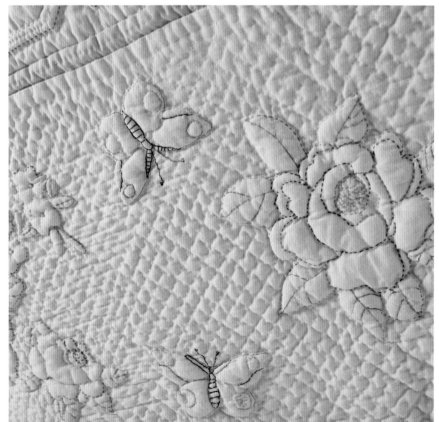

The wide border has a 1cm (½in) cross-hatch pattern for the final quilting, which contrasts with the high relief of the motifs.

The central design is stitched in running stitch using coloured thread, with the rose centres in seeding stitch. Another of my patterns, 'Ribbon Roses', has been adapted within the borders. We added the butterflies to give lightness to the design and to create a feeling of movement.

131

Rhapsody in Green

▶ 216 x 216cm (85 x 85in), BY SEN ARPINO

Sen used my 41cm (16in) 'Malvern Glory' pillow pattern for this, her first quilt, made from gold and green shot silk with matching gold silk accents. When the Malvern blocks are joined together my 'Malvern Spring' design appears. For the corners of the central panel, Sen used my 'Ivory Echo' pattern. A plain gold silk narrow border divides the main body of the quilt from the border. Here the use of half of the 'Echo' pattern makes an interesting border, which works well with the centre. There is a final 6cm (2½in) gold silk border that folds over to the back of the quilt, eliminating the need to bind the edges and giving the same size border on the back. The quilt features 1cm (½in) cross-hatch diagonal quilting and is embellished with self-coloured covered buttons. It is hand-stitched and quilted, and machine-pieced. This rich and sumptuous looking quilt is also backed with gold silk.

The completed quilt.

132

This narrow gold border edges the central patterns. Gold-coloured covered buttons are used along the outer border.

The 'Malvern Glory' block.

My 'Malvern Spring' design appears when the blocks are joined without sashing. Self-coloured covered buttons are added where the blocks are joined together to echo the centre of the motif in the 'Glory' block.

133

Ignorance is Bliss

▶ 140 x 140cm (55 x 55in),
BY CHRISTINE PARKER

This was the first quilt that Christine made with me. I ran a short course showing how to create the raised technique by using quilting stencils. Two different stencils were combined to make the finished nine-block quilt in dusky pink cotton fabric. The design did not require sashing as the alternating square incorporated a visual one in its design. Christine said that she didn't know what she had let herself in for when she joined the class and so the quilt was named accordingly! It was hand-stitched and hand-pieced with pearl embellishment.

The completed quilt.

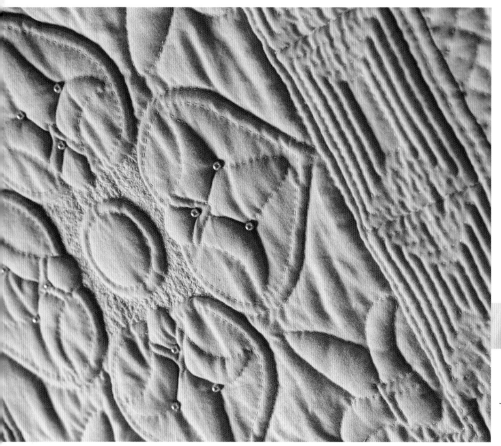

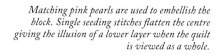

Matching pink pearls are used to embellish the block. Single seeding stitches flatten the centre giving the illusion of a lower layer when the quilt is viewed as a whole.

This angle shows how the raised work sculpts the surface of the fabric. The final quilting creates the dropped shadow which adds shading to the finished piece.

Carol's Quilt

▶ 244 x 360cm (96 x 142in), BY SUE IRWIN

Sue also attended my stencil quilting course, and this was the first quilt that she made with me. Her decision was to use only one of the stencils that I provided but to use the four alternatives that I suggested. Each block is 45cm (17½in) square; there are twenty-eight in total plus a 36cm (14in) border all around. The border design was developed from sections taken from the main block and each motif was linked to make a flowing design to complement the main body of the quilt. This is a magnificent king-size quilt with curved corners. It is machine-pieced, hand-stitched and quilted using the quilt-as-you-go method.

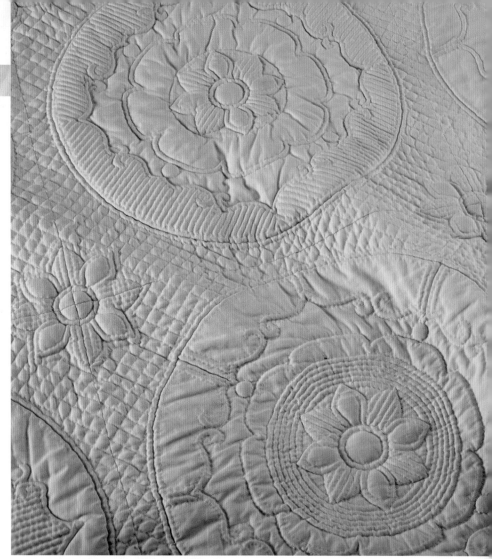

The two motifs alternate around the border and the connecting section is filled with parallel quilting in a diamond pattern, 4cm (1½in) apart. The diagonal quilting for the background of the border is 2.5cm (1in) apart. Changing the proportions of the cross-hatch quilting makes a far more interesting border. The quilt is finished with 2.5cm (1in) wide binding.

The images left and below show how the blocks differ in design. The background is quilted with 1cm (½in) cross-hatch diagonal quilting. A copy of the centre motif appears when four blocks are joined together and by alternating where the channels appear on the 'flower' petal – this helps to hide the join.

In a Spin

▶ 229 x 290cm (90 x 114in),
BY ANNIE SUMMERHAYES

This quilt began when Annie purchased an interesting blue and cream striped fabric. It started out as a Dresden plate design but the stripes proved to be a nightmare as they had a random ripple design throughout. Once made up, they looked a mess and the availability of the fabric was very limited, as tends to happen with all quilting fabrics. My solution was to photocopy some of the fabric and then, using a transparent template, selectively cut each segment for the plate from an identical area of the paper design. This way we could see how the final patchwork would look and whether it would look less messy. The result was striking but very busy and it wasted much of the fabric, resulting in only six plates, therefore I suggested we use a variation of my 'Ivory Inspiration' pattern for the remaining block. Annie was

open to my suggestion that we make each block individually and then lace them together with fine cord – much like a corset – through rouleaux loops.

Eventually this became a separate quilt, which is attached to the background quilt with covered buttons made from the remaining striped fabric. The background quilt has a centre that simply has squares quilted onto it that line up with the top quilt. These plates appear to spin and pulse when you view them in the quilt – very much like the 'Op Art' of the 1960s. The quilt has a narrow concertina design border of matching plain blue fabric and the left-overs of striped fabric. The final border is made up from all the remaining materials. It is both hand and machine-stitched and hand-quilted.

A 46cm (18in) raised quilt block completed with twenty handmade rouleaux loops.

Here you can see the fine cord laced intersections. Where the cords are tied off at the end of each row they are tied into bows and a small piece of the striped fabric is stitched decoratively onto each end to prevent it from fraying.

The border is edged either side with a 'flange' – a very narrow strip of plain blue material set into the seam to add a flash of colour without adding to the size of the quilt. This is similar to piping but without the cord inside.

Further inspiration

The following pages show a collection of my designs that I have made up to illustrate other ideas for using the techniques. All the patterns are available from my website if you want to try them out.

Camellia pillow

▷ 41 x 41cm (16 x 16in)

Made from cream calico (muslin), this pillow is stitched and quilted with cream silk-finish cotton sewing machine thread. Early spring always heralds stunning bright flower colours – a welcome change from the long grey days of winter. I particularly like the bright pink double flowers of the camellia shrubs and designed this pillow with that in mind. The final quilting gives the multi-layered effect typical of these blooms.

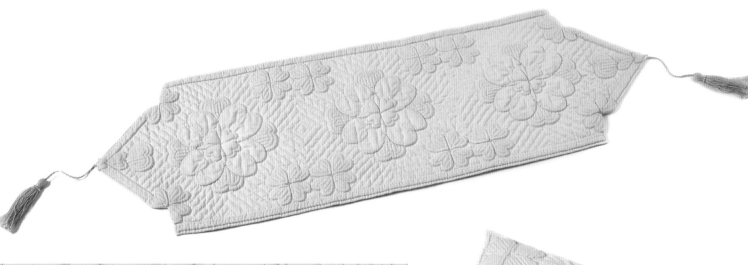

Summer Garden pillow and matching table runner

▷ PILLOW: 46 x 46cm (18 x 18in)
TABLE RUNNER: 104 x 33cm (41 x 13in)

The pillow border and runner background are echo quilted. Small pearl beads embellish the flower centres on both pieces and the shaped ends of the runner have handmade tassel, cord and bead embellishments. Both are made from cream calico (muslin).

Sixth Sense framed pictures

🔺 A SET OF THREE, EACH 30 x 30cm (12 x 12in)

Whilst watching the supernatural thriller *The Sixth Sense*, starring Bruce Willis and Hayley-Joel Osment, I noticed a scene where they were speaking together in a church in front of a large decorative window. The interesting pattern caught my eye, and as I always have my notebook to hand, I made a quick sketch of the outline. I later made several sketches varying the line design to produce these three designs. All the designs are made from cream calico (muslin).

Sixth Sense pincushions

◀ EACH 13 x 13cm (5 x 5in)

These three cream calico (muslin) pincushions are scaled-down versions of the above pictures. Pincushions are an ideal way to try out new techniques that might not be familiar to you.

Valentine pillow

▶ 43 x 43cm (17 x 17in)

This white calico (muslin) pillow is stitched with red running and backstitch for the main pattern, then quilted with white thread and some details in red. Using the red thread emphasises the Valentine theme. The parallel corded lines around the outer edge of the pillow eliminate the need to add a piped edge finish.

Night Moths pillow

▶ 28 x 25cm (15 x 10in)

This small shot silk pillow is made in the darkest tone that you should use with the raised technique, or else the dropped shadow effect becomes lost. The centre background is decorated with single seeding stitch, while double seeding quilting is sprinkled across the remaining background areas in silver metallic thread.

Flitterbugs pillow

◀ 46 x 46cm (18 x 18in)

The butterfly design is stitched with a variety of coloured threads in both polyester and silk-finish cotton. It contrasts completely with the Night Moths pillow above. All my designs work equally well with both coloured stitching and stitching that matches the background fabric. Running stitch and backstitch are used for the main design, which is quilted in the ditch. Double seeding is added at the final stage, with satin stitch beads used for the bugs' antennae; backstitch quilting is used for the caterpillars and plant tendrils.

Christmas Rose pincushion

▶ 13 x 13cm (5 x 5in)

The motif is stitched with backstitch in a variety of coloured threads. It includes double cross-stitch quilted stars, and is embellished with French knots in metallic threads. Beads and cold-fix half-pearls complete the festive design. This pattern could be used to make decorations for a Christmas tree: finish without the stuffing, mount on firm plastic and add a ribbon hanging loop on one corner.

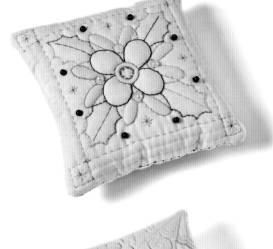

Retro 60s Arcs pillow

▶ 41 x 41cm (16 x 16in)

I designed this pattern during the 1960s for a piece of machine-embroidered lace. The original design is 15.25cm (6in) square. Upon revisiting it, I decided to scale it up to become the pillow that you see here. It is made from cream calico (muslin), with running stitch, stitch-in-the-ditch quilting, and double cross-stitch beads for the quilting in the background areas.

Sumatra pillow

◀ 41 x 41cm (16 x 16in)

Part of this design was inspired by a Sumatran house decoration carved from wood, and part from a small gift bag that I had kept from the 1970s – I keep anything that I find interesting! I mirror imaged the final ideas into a diagonal design on cream calico (muslin). The pillow features running stitch and backstitch, as well as bead embellishment.

From Little Acorns pillow

▶ 41 x 41cm (16 x 16in)

This design began life as a doodle I made whilst answering the phone. After scaling it up, I started stitching the centre of the pillow design on a 30 x 30cm (12 x 12in) piece of fabric but felt that it needed enlarging, so added the 6cm (2½in) border with mitred corners. Putting the oak leaf pattern on the corners allowed me to hide the join by using the leaf vein as part of the design. There is a mixture of techniques and finishes on this piece, and I used bullion knots for the detail on the acorns.

The matching acorn pincushion is a scaled-down version of the original pillow centre. As it is so much smaller, I stitched it with backstitch so that the detail was not lost, and used laidwork to represent the acorn cups.

From Little Acorns pincushion

▶ 13 x 13cm (5 x 5in)

Dicentra waistcoat

◀ UK SIZE 10–12

The *Dicentra* 'Purple Aurora' plant was my inspiration for the design that flows across the waistcoat from the front to the back in a continuous pattern. It is made from one piece of cream calico (muslin) with rouleaux and antique button fastenings on the shoulders, with twisted rouleaux for the front button closures. The tassels are optional: they are attached onto buttons so they can easily be removed. Split stitch stamens, tiny pearl buttons and small beads are embellished across the piece. Lined with matching wild silk dupion. This could easily become an interesting wall hanging when opened out flat (see page 144).

143